Material Cultures in Public Engagement

Re-inventing public archaeology within museum collections

edited by

Anastasia Christophilopoulou

OXBOW | books

Oxford & Philadelphia

Published in the United Kingdom in 2020 by
OXBOW BOOKS
The Old Music Hall, 106–108 Cowley Road, Oxford OX4 1JE

and in the United States by
OXBOW BOOKS
1950 Lawrence Road, Havertown, PA 19083

Paperback Edition: ISBN 978-1-78925-368-9
Digital Edition: ISBN 978-1-78925-369-6 (ePub)

A CIP record for this book is available from the British Library

Library of Congress Control Number: 2020941563

Printed in the United Kingdom by Short Run Press

Typeset by Versatile PreMedia Services (P) Ltd.

For a complete list of Oxbow titles, please contact:

UNITED KINGDOM
Oxbow Books
Telephone (01865) 241249
Email: oxbow@oxbowbooks.com
www.oxbowbooks.com

UNITED STATES OF AMERICA
Oxbow Books
Telephone (610) 853-9131, Fax (610) 853-9146
Email: queries@casemateacademic.com
www.casemateacademic.com/oxbow

Oxbow Books is part of the Casemate Group

Front and back cover: Images © the Fitzwilliam Museum 2020.

The past is seen and touched and tasted and smelt as well as heard and read about. Empathy, re-enactment, memory and commemoration overwhelm traditional history

David Lowenthal: *The Past as a Foreign Country*

For Lucilla
With gratitude for her endless support and encouragement
And to our Fitzwilliam Museum 'frontline' learning and public engagement
practitioners for making every day, the past, less of a 'foreign country'

Contents

D. Conclusions

Acknowledgements

My interest in producing this volume begun during my years as a field archaeologist, particularly those months spent excavating in remote places in Greece. There, fascinated about the finds that would appear before my eyes, I contemplated how much of this heritage would be accessible and offered to debate by the wider public. Public Archaeology was not a subject taught at University in Greece, during my early studies, but anyone involved with the archaeological field at an early stage soon finds him/herself a mediator of the past we excavate, reshape, and bequeath to the future.

In Cambridge, as a museum curator, I found myself on the other side. The public was there now and my task (particularly during my first assignment for the Fitzwilliam Museum) was to make museum exhibits accessible and relevant to our audiences. What was missing now, however, was the 'stage', the archaeological landscape and context that surrounded these objects and had shaped so much of my early experiences. How was I to talk about these objects to people who had not witnessed it?

This volume is, therefore, the product of my *shared* experience with archaeology and material culture studies. An experience shaped by interaction with other researchers in archaeology, heritage and material culture studies; field archaeologists; museum curators and of course museum educators, outreach and public engagement practitioners. We all come from very different backgrounds and very different realities have shaped our experience with heritage. But we are all equally preoccupied with communicating the past to the public and through this process, practitioners, academics and the public alike, we interpret it to serve our present needs and future hopes, and we construe our collective and individual heritage identities.

In the words of David Lowenthal: 'The past is past, but survives in and all around us, indispensable and inescapable'. Much inspiration has been drawn from his work during the production of this book, particularly from his seminal work *The Past as a Foreign Country* (Cambridge, 1985). Lucilla Burn, to whom this book is dedicated, enabled the work that inspired this book and co-organised with me the 2015 *Material Cultures in Public Engagement* conference in Cambridge, which brought the group of this volume's contributors together for the first time. Most of all, Lucilla provided invaluable support, encouragement and intellectual stimulus to all my endeavours over the past ten years and continues to do so today. I am truly indebted to her.

The Topoi Excellence Cluster and the Berliner Antike-Kolleg provided me with fellowships in Belin during 2009–2010 and 2015 and I am indebted to their support as institutions, as well as to Dr Hauke Ziemssen and Dr Regina Attula in particular, for their support and encouragement. The Topoi Excellence Cluster additionally supported the 2015 conference financially, enabling colleagues and contributors to this volume from Germany to participate in the Cambridge conference. My time in Berlin during both fellowships provided me with much intellectual support and academic stimulus to further this book project. I am also very grateful to Christine Gerbich, a passionate practitioner and researcher in public archaeology and museums, organiser of the *Digging for the Future – In Dialogue about Archaeology and the Public* Symposium in Berlin during September 2015, for discussing early versions of this edited volume and providing much-valued remarks.

This volume includes contributions from 11 different institutions: national and regional museums, museums connected with emblematic archaeological sites, University Museums and Collections, as well as academic faculties and research institutions; across the United Kingdom, Germany and Greece. As this volume was never intended as the publication of the proceedings of the conference that first brought together this group, the time elapsed between the conference and the publication of this volume, enabled many of us to form multiple synergies and promote discussions around the theme of public participation with the material cultures of the ancient world. I am therefore grateful to our contributors, not only for being part of this volume but for also making a contribution where it matters: the practice of public engagement.

Among the contributors, Professor Nena Galanidou and Professor Robin Osborne, both continuous advisors and sources of endless support to my career from my postgraduate studies to today, deserve a special mention. To be able to host their contributions in this volume is an honour. I am further grateful to Professor Carrie Vout for invaluable discussions on ancient material culture and to Professor Cyprian Broodbank for providing much academic support over the last four years.

I am further truly thankful to the following people: Dr Miranda Stearn for reading and making vital comments to versions of the introduction and my contribution; as well as the entire Learning Department of the Fitzwilliam Museum for making public engagement, practice, every day in the museum. They are an exemplary team of public engagement ambassadors, and for this reason, this book is also dedicated to them. My colleagues in the Department of Antiquities, for their support and encouragement during the preparation of this book; particularly Jennifer Marchant who has diligently prepared the objects used for our public handling sessions, and whose untimely death now leaves a great void in our Department; Daniel Pett and Dr Jennifer Wrexler, for enabling the fascinating digital content discussed in my chapter contribution; Michal Jones and the entire Image library team of the Fitzwilliam Museum for providing all images from the Fitzwilliam in this publication; Dr Susanne Turner and Dr Andrew Shapland for allowing photographic material from the Museum of Classical Archaeology, Cambridge and the Ashmolean Museum, Oxford respectively; Dr Jo Vine, our Research Facilitator for her support and encouragement with academic outputs during the past three years. My student, Rafael Laoutaris, for participating in our public engagement and handling sessions and for fruitful discussions on engaging our museum audiences to our favourite group of the collections, the Cypriot Antiquities. Jack Stephenson for diligently preparing and contributing to a large number of public and student-oriented sessions during this academic year.

Last but not least I am truly grateful to our varied audiences and communities in the Fitzwilliam as it is thanks to the interaction with them, that this project, public actions and edited volume were shaped and evolved.

Summary

Material Cultures in Public Engagement seeks to document and explore significant changes in the relationship of Museums with Ancient World collections with their audiences. It establishes a new approach to the study of public archaeology as a discipline and application within Museums, by bringing together the voices and experiences of museum professionals (curators, conservators and researchers) and public engagement professionals. Chapters in this volume present clear case-studies of the variety and diversity of public engagement projects conducted currently with European Museums and beyond. While the majority of case studies presented here stem from European museum programmes reference is also made to parallel strategies and successful public engagement programmes outside Europe. Case studies within the volume provide important insights as to why public engagement programmes have developed in different ways in Europe and the Americas, as well as to whether these differences may stem from different curatorial practices. And several studies included in this volume point out that methodologies and practices of public engagement applied currently by museums in or outside Europe, are rarely the subject of theoretical and methodological scrutiny, unlike other fields of study of the Ancient World or other social sciences. In summary, chapters within the book promise to contribute to the advancement of public engagement with the Ancient World, as well as to the advancement of public archaeology itself.

A. Theoretical Principles and Challenges

Chapter 1

Introduction: Public Archaeology Initiatives within Museum Spaces

Anastasia Christophilopoulou and Lucilla Burn

How do we Define Public Archaeology?

Public engagement with archaeology is often referred to as the practice of involving the public with archaeological, historical and art-historical evidence and associated interpretations. It is also known as the practice of familiarising the public with the methodologies employed by practitioners in the field of archaeology and related disciplines. It seeks to engage the interest of the public, passing on either specialist knowledge in an accessible form, or glimpses of the experience and challenges faced by curators, archaeologists and art historians in their own line of work. Public Archaeology is a complex and challenging field of archaeology. For many researchers, it is a trend within archaeology and not a distinct direction of the overall discipline, with its own theories, practices and quests (Moshenska 2017). Some, though, defend the existence of Public Archaeology as a separate theoretical direction in archaeology, as well as the need to integrate it as an essential part of its teaching in universities.

Public Archaeology, as either a theoretical or practical division of archaeology, was not first developed in the museum sphere, or for the needs of museum audiences; it was not even developed in universities as a theoretical direction. The first concepts of Public Archaeology and their subsequent consolidation into a theoretical branch of archaeology came about through the relationship of the public either with previously excavated archaeological monuments or with places under excavation that attracted the interest of those living near them. Public Archaeology was initially, and still is for many today, identified with the concept of 'Community Archaeology'. Although today this concept is intertwined with practices adopted in a large number of European, American and, more recently, African countries, it is the contribution of two specific countries that has established its direction in terms of both theory and practice. These countries are the United States of America and the United Kingdom.

In the United States, 'Archaeology for the Community' involves three different research and practice strands: (a) Community Archaeology programmes in cooperation with American indigenous communities; (b) collaborative programmes with other local and descendant communities; and (c) extensive public education programmes of cultural and environmental heritage issues. The first of these categories is perhaps the most important, as it was created to bridge a long history of social struggles that arose after numerous excavations of American indigenous sites were conducted without the agreement of the populations descending from them. Similarly, Community Archaeology programmes with other aboriginal descendant communities or communities of the (mainly African) diaspora were created to highlight and, where possible, resolve racial issues and issues of social separation within these communities, for example, stories of slavery and social segregation (Watkins 2006, xi). It is evident that, in the case of American Public Archaeology, both its strategy and practices are fully linked to the anthropological research programmes of the United States, particularly during the decades of 1950–1970. In terms of social impact, the implementation of Public Archaeology programmes has greatly helped these societies to redefine themselves to their cultural heritage, in a spirit of cohabitation rather than violence (Watkins 2003, 134).

The application of Public Archaeology in the United Kingdom has an even longer history. However, only in recent decades have the activities involved been described explicitly as archaeology for the Community or Public Archaeology. The fact that the practice and study of Public Archaeology have now entered British universities as a systematically taught curriculum unit has also facilitated the study of the history and evolution of the discipline, at least in the context of the United Kingdom. For Britain, the roots of Public Archaeology date back to the tradition of British collectors, as well as to the creation of local history and archaeology societies that began to exist as early as the onset of the 20th century (Trigger 2007).

These societies played an important role in encouraging public participation in archaeology. Until 1970, volunteers were able to organise or participate fully in excavations in their area, a possibility which was significantly reduced after that date with the development of professional and commercial archaeology companies, who were no longer permitted, for insurance reasons, to involve the public to participate in the excavation process (Moshenska 2009). After the establishment of systematic legislation on archaeological processes for the United Kingdom (Planning Policy Guidance note 16, *PPG*16), public participation in excavations has been further restricted (Merriman 2004, 1–17). However, the practice of Community Archaeology is very well established in the United Kingdom as compared to other European countries (Moshenska & Dhanjal 2012). The numerous popular local history and archaeology groups today in the United Kingdom display impressive results that reflect the public's level of participation, as well as the time and the effort dedicated by volunteers (Faulkner 2000, 21–33).

In the United Kingdom, further permanent posts of 'community archaeologists' that 'guarantee the development and strengthening of public participation at the local level' (Farley 2003, 14) have been created by the government. A typical case study is Leicestershire, where one of the most successful Public Archaeology projects was established in 1976 and today lists over 400 active members, 20 local archaeology groups and, most importantly, the first Museum curator (Keeper of Archaeology) who also holds the title of Community Archaeologist (Liddle 1985). The establishment of Public Archaeology, both in the United Kingdom and in the United States of America, has been a significant development both in the way in which archaeological data may now be accessed by the general public but also for how archaeology now interacts with the general public as social science with the potential to influence daily life, like other social sciences such as sociology, history and psychology/psychoanalysis.

The subsequent gradual introduction of Public Archaeology into the way of thinking and practice of other European museums, for example, those in Germany, Greece and Italy, is an essential factor in the development of their public programmes, as well as in the way in which they now self-identify as museums. Although the theoretical and practical directions of archaeology in these three countries are quite different, their correlation here has to do with the strong presence of the state in the way the discipline of archaeology operates in these countries; the way museums are organised and function; and finally, the influence of legislation regulating public participation in museums and heritage (Matsuda 2004, 66–76). A few case-studies may illustrate this relationship. In Greece, legislation governing archaeological procedures and safeguarding of heritage does not allow private individuals to be involved in its processes, such as archaeological surveys, excavations and archaeological studies, including publications. Consequently, the decades-long established relationship between local community initiatives and archaeology in the United Kingdom – which allows citizens not only to participate in excavations or local museums as volunteers but also to shape the relationship between the discipline of archaeology and the state directives surrounding it – does not prevail in Greece. When public participation in the management of cultural heritage, as well as in the decision-making related to local historical and archaeological monuments is reduced, the likelihood of the public feeling alienated from their cultural heritage and ultimately not wanting to engage in protecting it actively, grows exponentially. The possibility lost here is what Faulkner (2000, 21–22) described in his seminal article 'Archaeology from below: a socialist perspective': 'Allowing public participation in archaeological research is a point of convergence between academic practice and everyday people – a point at which history is accessible directly to the masses'. However, contributions to this volume by museum directors, curators, educators and public engagement specialists representing the National Archaeological Museum of Greece and Athens' Acropolis Museum, indicate a variety of successful 'paradigm shifts', illustrating how museums can innovate in public engagement even before substantial changes are seen in legislation, or the relationship of the State with the discipline of archaeology.

Similar challenges exist in the theory and practice of Public Archaeology in Italy. As in Greece, the term Public Archaeology (Archeologia Pubblica) was not established by Italian researchers before 2000, and when it did emerge, it was through the interaction of Italian researchers with the theoretical advances made in Britain. However, over the last ten years, interest in Italy in Public Archaeology has increased, as confirmed by the participation of Italian archaeologists and museum curators alike in recent Public Archaeology conferences in Italy (Vannini & Nucciotti 2009; Bonacchi 2013; Zuanni 2013, 134–38). These conferences produced some ground-breaking views: Margherita Corrado, for example, showed how the participation of people from socially vulnerable groups in the Crotone region of Southern Italy, where she conducts excavations, can prove beneficial both for the local community and for the practice of archaeology in the region (Bonacchi 2009, 329–50).

The result of these conferences has shaped Public Archaeology in Italy as the 'Study and strengthening of the role of archaeology, as a historical science, and the interpretation and management of archaeological resources in order to benefit society and its development' (Bonacchi 2011, 103–4). This definition was subsequently proposed to the Italian Ministry for Culture, as well as the Ministry for Scientific Research and Education. Today, even though the application of Public Archaeology in Italy is not yet widely established, essential steps are being taken with its introduction as a discipline within universities. The application of Public Archaeology can be a way for Italian archaeologists not only to strengthen the protection of monuments and heritage sites they oversee but also to enhance public value and recognition of their profession.

It is clear, therefore, that Public Archaeology was initially developed as part of an attempt to preserve and maintain heritage and archaeological sites. However, a large part of today's public engagement in archaeology now centres on museums. This relationship is further strengthened by the fact that many large European Art and Antiquities collections have been assembled and are maintained with public funds (in the case of major state museums in Greece, Germany and Italy – also illustrated by case studies in this volume – this relationship is even more apparent) and therefore the responsibility of their curators and museum practitioners to 'give back' to the public their collections, via learning resources and public engagement activities, is of prime importance. For many museums, this change of direction, from inward-looking institutions to those that seek a more dialectic and dynamic relationship with their audiences, does not simply derive from their curatorial/learning practitioners being more sensitive to issues of public engagement but is also the result of fundamental changes in the way their public now perceives and experiences the ancient world. In other words, change seems to be happening 'from below', just as it was a few decades ago with the dawn of Public Archaeology.

Improved accessibility to material culture from the ancient world, due to technological progress (including, for example, advances in digital archaeology, the rise of the 'virtual museum', or tactile 3-D reconstructed collections), as well as the public's increased ability to travel to the source countries of ancient world collections, have together led to significant changes in the ways we perceive, engage and experience the ancient world. Museum curators, educators, and other museum professionals are suddenly faced with the challenge of how best to exploit these changes and opportunities, to create appropriate activities and programmes that will both reflect their collections and inspire different audiences to visit them. Even more, perhaps, they are concerned about how to 'translate' their ancient world narratives (narratives previously often based on academic vocabulary and way of thinking), into narratives and interpretations understood by the wider public and relevant to their everyday experiences. Again, several contributions in this volume (for example case studies from the Fitzwilliam Museum and the Museum of Archaeology and Anthropology, Cambridge) concern themselves with creating the right balance between analogue and digital resources to support the visitor's experience. And nearly all contributors to this volume acknowledge the public's need and right to curate one's own experience, by being able to access and focus on the information that interests them as individuals. For museum professionals what looks already like a challenging task becomes more complicated when it is unclear whose competence is the greater in facing these challenges.

The points discussed above are necessary to comprehend better how Public Archaeology and its evolution have influenced museum theory and practice. We may now turn to specific European museum case studies from Germany, Greece and the United Kingdom that demonstrate this change, either as a result of early exposure to Public Archaeology and its practice or through the more recent introduction of its theory and practice to museum thinking and programming. The aim is not to produce an exhaustive description of all kinds of museum programmes and actions undertaken within this framework, but rather to shed light on the evolving relationship between Public Archaeology and museums that identify as university museums, national museums, or with links to specific heritage sites.

Past and Present Public Archaeology and Public Engagement Efforts within European Museums

One of the questions this volume seeks to explore is the extent to which public engagement with the ancient world is actively pursued in current European museum practice. Here we may explore this through three distinct categories of museums: university museums; large national museums; and museums linked to emblematic historic and archaeological sites. To the first category belong such British university museums as the Fitzwilliam Museum and the Museum of Archaeology and Anthropology in Cambridge, and Oxford's Ashmolean Museum; in the second category are found such large national museums as the Antikensammlung and Neues Museum in Germany, as well as the National Archaeological Museum of Athens; while in the third category of museums connected to significant archaeological sites, we discuss the Acropolis Museum in Athens.

Figure 1.1: The entrance and part of the staircase of the Ashmolean Museum, after its full refurbishment, completed in November 2009. The museum's new concept 'connecting worlds, connecting cultures' allows the visitor to experience collections using crossovers between different chronological and geographical regions (image: The Ashmolean Museum, 2020).

In terms of university museums, our emphasis has been on museums within the United Kingdom. The existence of university museums in Europe is attested as early as the end of the 17th century, a notable example being the establishment of the Ashmolean Museum in Oxford in 1683 (MacGregor 2001) (Fig. 1.1). It was followed by the establishment of the Fitzwilliam Museum in Cambridge, founded in 1816 (Burn 2016, 1–3 & 60–3). Since the founding of the first university museum (Ashmolean) to date, university museums in Britain have achieved over 300 years of collecting, displaying, researching and teaching their collections. The changes that occurred between the 17th and 21st centuries in terms of teaching, scientific advances and understanding of the natural and ancient world within those universities that include museums had a very significant impact on the kind of collections that were created, how these collections were preserved and conserved, as well as how they were displayed. Two illustrations may be offered from the Fitzwilliam Museum: an important part of museum's Cypriot collection was created as a result of the late 19th-century founding of the Cyprus Exploration Society. This association conducted excavations and promoted the study of Cypriot archaeology with the participation of Cambridge researchers. Around the same time (1884) the Fitzwilliam decided to split the antiquities collections from its plaster casts and create a separate museum, the Museum of Classical Archaeology (also known as the Cast Gallery), not just because of lack of space but because of revised opinions as to what was appropriate for display in the Fitzwilliam (Burn 2016, 104–5). In this volume, contributions illustrate precisely this relationship, that is, how the theoretical approaches and debates that have taken place at major European universities over the last three centuries have directly influenced the development and display strategies of their associated or embedded museums (MacGregor 2001).

Going forward, the identity of a university museum, forged through its relationship with its parent university, has a direct influence on the way it develops its public engagement strategy and programming today (Boylan 1999). If we compare the present-day integration and practice of public participation in university museums we will observe significant differences, many due to the identity of the parent university.

The transition from the traditional role of a university museum (maintaining and augmenting collections with a strong research interest, for example, focusing on providing collections-based teaching or supporting relevant university classes) to a programme addressing the needs of the wider public, is challenging and time-consuming. The task becomes even harder if the ambition extends to laying the ground for the active participation of those historically less likely to visit, for example vulnerable social groups and individuals, groups with learning disabilities, or LGBTQ and BAME communities. Often the well-established (if not traditional) identity of the institution can be an inhibiting factor. For example, all eight Cambridge University museums, despite their active efforts to provide a multivocality of public engagement activities, still struggle with the widespread and enduring perception that their collections can only speak to the academic community or specialised researchers.

Specific examples of recent actions and programmes from university museums in this volume demonstrate new initiatives in public engagement as well as the challenges and adversities faced while implementing them by curators, public

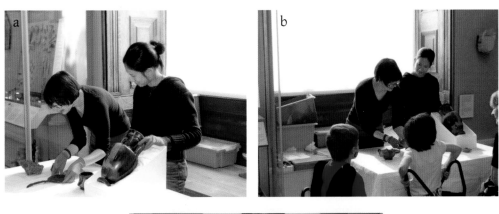

Figure 1.2: a–b: Public engagement programmes with the material culture of the ancient world; c: programmes aimed at families (images: Fitzwilliam Museum, 2020).

engagement and learning specialists or other museum professionals. Our own experience in the Fitzwilliam Museum (at least over the past decade) has exposed many of these challenges but has also revealed pathways that can lead to new approaches. Emerging opportunities include the importance of engaging with ancient material culture as a point of contact for the public with the ancient world; the importance of incorporating sensory experiences for young children and adults within the museum environment; as well as challenges such as the realisation that public engagement in museum practice should be regarded as a fundamental professional task rather than an add-on activity, paired with the fact that 'we are not there yet' in establishing this practice. Three of the Fitzwilliam's programmes, implemented between 2010 and 2020, acted as beacons for continuing these efforts and overcoming challenges. In 2011, the Fitzwilliam initiated a new programme for disability groups, particularly for blind and visually impaired people, launched as a series of 'blind and tactile tours' of specific objects across the Greek, Roman and Cypriot collection (Fig. 1.2a–c). The project developed gradually over a decade and required a lot of adjustment by a plethora of professionals across and outside the museum. Still, today it is established and has been extended to other curatorial departments as well and is hailed as one of the museum's most inclusive and impactful public programmes. Another successful public intervention was the creation of a 'Live' conservation laboratory as part of the 2016 exhibition *Death on the Nile*. Here museum visitors were able to watch live and at close quarters the process of analysing the colours with which ancient wooden Egyptian coffins were decorated and, at the same time, to understand how research questions and methods used in conservation are an essential element in answering questions about the context, technology and making, as well as function of the ancient objects. (Fig. 1.3a–b). However, the Fitzwilliam's most ground-breaking action over the past decade was a learning resource programme focused on Ancient Egypt, created by Dr Sally-Ann Ashton (Egyptologist and Assistant Keeper of Antiquities) tailored for and targeted at young BAME offenders. This programme was conducted exclusively in prisons around the country. It took the form of seminars and workshops on African-based Egyptology, enabling participants to participate in vocational training and ultimately contributing to their post-release reintegration into society.

Examining the category of major national museums, this volume explores, among others, the example of the Antikensammlung and the Neues Museum in Berlin. The Antikensammlung, which comprises three different museums (Pergamon, Asiatisches Museum and the Bode Museum), as well as the Neues Museum, was partly destroyed during the Second World War and the subsequent separation between West and East Germany. Reconstruction began immediately after the reunification of Germany in 1990 and continued with a multi-layered and ambitious project which includes not only the renovation of the four museums but also their connection through a new Hall (the James Simon gallery). The example of the Neues Museum is striking: this museum, through its successful renovation, renegotiated its relationship with the history of the city, demonstrated the history of its building, and ultimately constructed

Figure 1.3: 'Live' conservation workshop during the exhibition Death on the Nile, *Fitzwilliam Museum 2016 (images: Fitzwilliam Museum, 2016).*

new relationships with new audiences (Fig. 1.4). The history of these collections, their partial destruction during the war, and their division into eastern and western collections is fittingly presented through new displays and galleries in the characteristically honest way modern German museum practice has dealt with the country's complicated past. What has been achieved here is that new narratives and displays have incorporated elements that promote a dialectic relationship between the museum's new audiences, the museum's history and its renewed public engagements priorities.

In the final museum category examined within this volume, two emblematic national museums present their case studies and public engagement strategies, without shying away from the challenges that occur when planning and delivering these programmes. The archaeological site of the Athenian Acropolis and the New Acropolis Museum could not offer a more perfect example of the new opportunities arising from engaging the public with an ancient site of such crucial archaeological, historical and national significance. At the same time, the two case studies presented by the National Archaeological Museum of Athens alert us to the

Figure 1.4: East façade of the Berlin New Museum (Neues Museum) (image: Staatliche Museen zu Berlin, Museum für Vor- und Frühgeschichte, photo by Achim Kleuker, 2017).

fact that national archaeological museums (and museums accompanying major archaeological sites) are still perceived as traditional and static entities and can also be challenged by the lack of meaning-making possibilities, despite their rich and unique collections.

Public Archaeology and Museum Identity: Towards a New Dialogue?

Building on the previous assumptions, how can we ensure progress in the dialectic relationship between museums and their now 'complex' audiences? And, most importantly, how can museums integrate social participation and public engagement practices into their core operations and not see them as a mere 'add-on' to their traditional activities? At present, there exists limited theoretical debate on how this can be achieved. In essence, we need more discussion, more dialogue between museum curators and museum educators, more conferences, bringing together both the experiences of archaeologists, curators, researchers, conservators and museum learning specialists and also their concerns about how fast this discipline is evolving and how difficult it is to align museum practices and operations with the pace of this change.

Museum-based researchers and curators have seen in recent years their role descriptions changing dramatically. Beyond their core tasks of curating displays and exhibitions, researching their collections, maintaining and safeguarding them, they now face increased responsibilities that come with public engagement tasks. New generations of museum professionals are welcoming these new roles within their job descriptions and are even further welcoming newly established financial investment specifically tied to commitments and aspirations around public engagement, provided by academic, public or charitable funding bodies. Several contributors in this volume testify, through their recently implemented case studies, to their commitment to diversifying audiences and embracing forms of public engagement as part of their core tasks.

What further positive steps can be taken to increase public engagement in museums, while at the same time admitting that very rapid changes are not easy to implement? One of the points addressed by several contributors in this volume touches on museum exhibition strategies and how these can be aligned with current and future public engagement priorities and aspirations. This is an important point given that, until recently, major exhibitions across Europe and America were usually designed without any consideration of learning and public engagement impact and outcomes. A substantial change, however, may be documented over the past ten years, with exhibition projects designed not just to include public engagement outcomes but also with public engagement and public co-curation as the central theme or aim of the show, a point made by three contributors to this volume. The process of this change is not straightforward, though, and it requires allocation of internal resources, funding and creative thinking across a variety of museum disciplines, including the need to over-ride the notion that exhibition projects are solely created and managed

by curators, museum directors and researchers. In other words, exhibition programming, frequently one of the most important operations of a museum, needs to
be integrated into that museum's participation strategy and its commitment to its
audiences. Substantial changes have also been noted in the way museum projects and
exhibitions are now evaluated, with impact, learning and community engagement
being almost as important outcomes as research goals and achievements.

Many emblematic 'national' museums, museums which traditionally and until
recently served to confirm or establish a nation's identity through the collection and
display of ancient or modern material culture, now also feel the need to reinvent – or
at least readjust – their identity and orientation. It is now clear that their audiences
are no longer mono-dimensional or representative of just one nation, but diverse,
multicultural and constantly evolving. An interesting example of this phenomenon is
provided by the national museums in Greece where, until recently, museum audiences
were mostly of a single ethnic origin. Lately, though, the Greek museum-going public
has become increasingly multicultural and multifaith, including a growing number of
immigrants and refugees. The fact that a significant percentage of the Greek popula-
tion between the ages of 20 and 75 is now or has been educated abroad has also resulted
in widespread exposure to other cultures and generally increased diversification. One
consequence of this is the need for permanent collections, temporary exhibitions and
learning/outreach activities and programmes to respond to new quests, aspirations
and concerns. Public engagement strategy of these museums must now be drawn up
by a collaborative team in which curators work alongside archaeologists, exhibition
officers, learning and public engagement specialists, abandoning the old practice of
the museum curator dictating a narrative to the museum audience.

On the other hand, museums connected with flagship archaeological sites, privileged to display narratives combining architectural and other contextual data with
their concomitant material culture(s), can use this opportunity to explore another
level: there is now keen public interest in the history of excavations and the evolution of the disciplines of archaeology and conservation; interest in the biographies of archaeologists who discovered these sites; and also in the evolution of the
surrounding landscape and communities. In other words, the public demands that
these museums become communicators of the process and the 'philosophy' of the
discipline of archaeology and not just its results. An excellent example of how this
has been achieved in a museum context is offered by the Aegean World galleries in
Oxford's Ashmolean museum, curated by Dr Yiannis Galanakis (Fig. 1.5). Here, within
the framework of current academic priorities of Aegean Archaeology, Galanakis has
successfully integrated the history of excavations of the emblematic site of Knossos
with the material culture excavated there and subsequently transferred to Oxford
by Sir Arthur Evans.

Reference to the Ashmolean Museum brings us to the last museum category
discussed under this volume: university museums. University Museums have an
equally vital role to play, as by their very nature they are ambassadors, or indeed

Figure 1.5: The Aegean World galleries, Ashmolean Museum (image: The Ashmolean Museum, 2020).

shop-windows, for the knowledge, research and scientific discoveries generated in their universities. Their narratives are not only limited to the history of the objects in their collections but may also involve the stories of their discovery and the persons associated with it. They may often describe the evolution of discipline around the subject (archaeology, geology, natural sciences) represented in their collections. Their dual nature is now called to respond to a bigger challenge, which is to make their narratives interesting and engaging to the wider public and not just their traditional audience of researchers, academics and university students (Lourenço 2004, 1–12). Two promising directions begin to take shape as the result of recent experiences of European university museums: the attempt to connect with the local, non-university, communities and their needs and aspirations and the engaging dissemination of university-derived scientific methods and results to the public. With their long experience, university museums have both the material and the knowledge to inspire the public and play a leading part in developing museums that are dynamically connected to society (Warhurst 1986, 137–40).

In this introduction, we have explored the importance of empowering the public so that they can feel connected to and able to engage with their cultural heritage, including items of material culture housed in museums. We have described how the onset of Public Archaeology as a discipline was based on the movement of 'archaeology from below'; how the change in the way museum engagement programmes and activities are designed and conducted is based on the public's needs and aspirations (audience-driven engagement); and how evaluation of museum engagement programmes is also now a way to measure the public impact of sciences and disciplines associated with archaeology (impact studies in archaeology, history and anthropology). If we were to identify a theme common to all contributions in this volume, it would be to echo the aspirations Professor Themelis recently voiced in his article 'Open and Engaging Museums and Archaeological Sites' (Themelis 2017): 'in order to promote the public's awareness and engagement with their cultural heritage, we must first give those who are active in the field of culture (museum curators, researchers, university professors, field archaeologists) the space and opportunity to develop and innovate in this direction; in other words other than just accepting an 'archaeology from below', a deep endoscopic process is also required by those already working in the field of cultural heritage, museums and archaeological sites, to redefine their roles and priorities'. We hope this volume helps to pave the way in this direction.

References

Bonacchi, C. (2009) Archeologia pubblica in Italia. Origini e prospettive di un 'nuovo' settore disciplinare. *Ricerche Storiche*, 2–3, 329–50.

Bonacchi, C. (2011) Dalla Public Archaeology all'Archeologia Pubblica. La mostra Da Petra a Shawbak. In G. Vannini (ed.), *Archeologia Pubblica in Toscana: Un Progetto e una Proposta. Strumenti per la didattica e la ricerca,* 115, 1031–12. Florence, University Press.

Bonacchi, C. (2013) The development of Public Archaeology in Italy: a review of recent efforts. *Public Archaeology* 12(3), 211–16.

Boylan, P. (1999) Universities and museums: past, present and future. *Museum Management and Curatorship* 18(1), 435–6.

Burn L. (2016) *The Fitzwilliam Museum, a History.* London, Philip Wilson.

Farley, M. (2003) *Participating in the Past: the results of an investigation by a Council for British Archaeology Working Party.* Council for British Archaeology. https://new.archaeologyuk.org (accessed May 2017).

Faulkner, N. (2000) Archaeology from below. A socialist perspective. *Public Archaeology* 1, 21–33.

Liddle, P. (1985) *Community Archaeology: a fieldworker's handbook of organisation and techniques.* Leicester, Leicestershire Museums Publication 61.

Lourenço, M. (2004) 'Where past, present and future knowledge meet: An overview of university museums and collections in Europe'. Unpublished paper presented at *Atti Convegno d'Autunno dell'Associazione Nazionale Musei Scientifici, 'Il Patrimoni della Scienza, Le collezione di interesse storico'* Torino, November 10–12, 2004.

MacGregor, A. (2001) *The Ashmolean Museum: a brief history of the museum and its collections.* London, Jonathan Horne.

Matsuda, A. (2004) The concept of the 'public' and the aims of Public Archaeology. *Papers from the Institute of Archaeology* 15, 66–76.

Merriman, N. (ed.) (2004) *Public Archaeology.* London, Routledge.

Moshenska, G. (2009) Beyond the viewing platform: excavations and audiences. *Archaeological Review from Cambridge* 24(1), 39–53.

Moshenska, G. (ed.) (2017) *Key Concepts in Public Archaeology.* London, University College London Press.

Moshenska, G. & Dhanjal, S. (eds) (2012) *Community Archaeology: themes, methods and practices.* Oxford, Oxbow Books.

Themelis P. (2017) 'Ανοιχτά μουσεία και αρχαιολογικοί χώροι', δημοσίευμα στην εφημερίδα. *Eleftheria* 2 April 2017. https://www.diazoma.gr/θεατροπαιδεία/κείμενο-ομιλίας-καθ-κ-πέτρου-θέμελη-στ/.

Trigger, B. (2007) *A History of Archaeological Thought* (2nd ed.). New York, Cambridge University Press.

Vannini, G. & Nucciotti, M. (eds) (2009) *Da Petra a Shawbak. Archeologia di una Frontiera. Catalogo.* Firenze, Giunti.

Warhurst, A. (1986) Triple crisis in university museums. *Museums Journal* 86 (3), 1371–40.

Watkins, J. (2003) Archaeological ethics and American Indians. In L. J. Zimmerman, K. D. Vitelli & J. Hollowell-Zimmer (eds), *Ethical Issues in Archaeology.* Walnut Creek, CA, AltaMira, 130–41.

Watkins, J. (2006) Forward. In J. E. Kerber (ed.), *Cross-Cultural Collaboration: Native Peoples and archaeology in the northeastern United States,* xi–xvi. Lincoln & London, NE, University of Nebraska Press.

Zuanni, C. (2013) Review: Archeologia Pubblica in Italia. Florence, 2012. *Online Journal in Public Archaeology* 3, 134–8.

B. Public engagement in Museums and Archaeological Sites: A Survey of Case Studies

Chapter 2

Forty-five Years in Engaging the Public with the Restoration of the Acropolis of Athens

Vasiliki Eleftheriou, Eugenia Lembidaki and Irene Kaimara

Introduction

The Acropolis of Athens, a unique World Heritage architectural monument, included since 1987 in the UNESCO's World Heritage Sites List, offers a significant case for promoting a variety of public engagement activities related to its history, archaeology and conservation. The Acropolis Restoration Service (YSMA) is the special Service of the Hellenic Ministry of Culture and Sports responsible for planning, directing and overseeing the interventions on the Acropolis monuments, under the general supervision of the Committee for the Conservation of the Acropolis Monuments. After almost 45 years of restoration work (Fig. 2.1) that has been awarded four times by Europa Nostra, the Service continues today to raise public awareness of the importance of the protection of the Acropolis monuments.

This paper provides an overview of the methodology used to embed public involvement in the Service's practice. With the mediation of new technologies and a diverse range of interpretative tools, especially during the last 20 years, the Acropolis Restoration Service aims at increasing the interaction between heritage and the public. In this way, an alternative encounter between the heritage site (Acropolis monuments) and the public is developed that promotes the understanding of the site's archaeological and historical values. At the same time, it supports an encounter that has broader implications on the interaction of the public with the cultural, aesthetic, social, artistic, emotional and learning qualities of this emblematic site.

The first section of the paper outlines the importance of the tools used by the Acropolis Documentation Department to make the contents of the Documentation Archive accessible to the general public. The second section describes the variety of the learning activities implemented by the Information and Education Department. It illustrates – through a case study – its holistic educational approach to attract a wide range of audiences.

Figure 2.1: The Acropolis viewed from the northwest (image: T. Souvlakis, 2018, YSMA Archive).

Outreach Activities of the Documentation Department

The detailed recording of the condition of the Acropolis monuments, the thorough documentation of their restoration (anastylosis) and conservation works and the dissemination of the restoration activities to the scientific community and the public, constitute an integral part of the conservation and restoration plan implemented since 1975. This approach is in accordance with the codes of conduct defined by the international conventions for the restoration and conservation of monuments and monumental complexes (*The Venice Charter* 1964, article 16).

The Documentation Archive of the restoration interventions carried out in the Erechtheion, the Parthenon, the Propylaea, the Temple of Athena Nike and the Acropolis walls, includes today more than 300,000 documents, such as photographs, film reels, audio-visual material and magnetic tapes; topographic, photogrammetric and drawn surveys and mappings; notebooks, documentation of scattered architectural members, restoration reports and published scientific studies. The above material is systematically aggregated, to ensure that the future generations will not only be able to navigate through the history of the restorations but also clearly understand their philosophy.

All this valuable heritage content becomes accessible to the scientific community and the general public through the consistent publication of all conservation and restoration studies, as well as of the final reports on the completed works, realised since 1976 (40 volumes to date). This is complemented with the organisation of International Meetings on the Restoration of the Acropolis Monuments (six meetings to date), of which the proceedings have also been published. During the International Meetings, current intervention studies and works are presented to the specialists, to inform them and allow them to express their views on the proposed interventions and contribute to the final proposals.

Alongside these activities, workshops, lectures and exhibitions, the Documentation Department has also produced documentaries of the restoration works in action (Fig. 2.2). Since 2000 the Service has also provided the annual newsletter of *The Acropolis Restoration News*, in Greek and English, which serves to inform the scientific community and the general public about the progress of the works. It has provided further information on specific aspects arising in the course of restoration works. Additional activities targeting a wider audience involve information brochures and leaflets for the visitor of the Acropolis that are also produced in Braille. Moreover, bilingual signposts on the Acropolis area inform the visitors about the restoration works on the monuments.

Figure 2.2: View of the photography exhibition Chisel and Memory. The contribution of marble craftsmanship to the restoration of the Acropolis monuments *at the Acropolis Museum, 11 June 2019–31 January 2020 (image: T. Souvlakis, 2019, YSMA Archive).*

The advantage of digital technology has helped implement further activities, such as the production of films about the restoration interventions in stereoscopic (3D), which are projected in the 'Virtual Theatre' of the Acropolis Museum. Moreover, a series of web applications have been developed (Alexopoulos & Katsianis 2012; Eleftheriou & Lempidaki 2016), including the official website of the restoration interventions (http://www.ysma.gr), the *Virtual Tour of the Acropolis Monuments* (http://www.acropolisvirtualtour.gr/), the platform for making digital documentation products publicly available, such as orthophotomosaics and three-dimensional models of the monuments (Mavromati 2015) (http://www.acropolis-gis.ysma.gr) and the new YSMA Library Catalogue (https://ysma.openabekt.gr/el), which has been developed in collaboration with the Hellenic National Documentation Centre.

The *Virtual Tour of the Acropolis Monuments* is an online application, receiving more than 90,000 visitors per year using both desktop and mobile devices. It provides remote access to the archaeological site, enabling the visitor to walk through the monuments and have a glimpse of the ongoing restoration works. This is achieved through a series of successive viewpoints of the site, in which the visitor is provided with high-resolution images and panoramas of the Parthenon, the Propylaea, the Erechtheion, the temple of Athena Nike and orthophotographs of the exterior side of the walls surrounding the rock. Navigation is facilitated through an orientation map based on the orthophotomosaic ground plan of the Acropolis rock marking the locations of the viewpoints. The high-resolution images can be significantly enlarged so that the users can observe details that cannot be seen in an actual visit to the site. At the same time, descriptive information concerning the monuments and selected places of interest is being displayed.

A further database system has been developed since 1997 for the digital management of the Documentation Archive of the Acropolis Restoration works (Mallouchou-Tufano *et al.* 1990; 2003; Mallouchou-Tufano 1992; Mallouchou-Tufano & Alexopoulos 2007; Katsianis 2013). The database can present, via a three dimensional environment displaying (Alexopoulos 2010, 32–34) selected architectural fragments or larger parts of the Acropolis monuments, including archival material and information concerning their state of preservation and the interventions applied to them, including archives of automatic drawing (CAD) and audio-visual material. It constitutes the principal tool for the digital management of the Acropolis restoration documentation content, allowing access to scientific staff. With 186,000 entries to date, it is extremely valuable for the composition of restoration reports and scientific studies, as well as for the preparation of the final publication of the completed restoration projects (Alexopoulos 2012; Lempidaki 2015; Lempidaki *et al.* 2018; Petropoulou & Koutsadelis 2018). At the same time, the database system enabled the design of a web application, the Repository of the Acropolis Restoration Service (http://repository-ysma.ekt.gr), which has been developed in collaboration with the Hellenic National Documentation Centre funded by the National Strategic Reference Framework (NSRF-ESPA) 2007–2013.

The ultimate aim for developing this repository was to ensure that future generations will be able to access knowledge related to the Acropolis monuments and the works that have been implemented on them (Katsianis & Kamatsos 2016). Further selected documentation material from the restoration interventions on the Erechtheion (1979–1987) has become available to the public. It includes studies, notebooks, audiovisual material, as well as drawings and photographic material which can be found in the CD-ROM that accompanies the publication of the final report on the restoration project (Mallouchou-Tufano & Bouras 2012). The Repository will be systematically enriched with new material following the progress of the interventions.

Learning Activities of the Information and Education Department

The Education Department of any cultural organisation is the first link between the institution and the public. Heritage learning can be a way of making cultural heritage relevant to people, as well as a way of transforming individuals and society (Hansen 2014, 7).

The educational activities of the Information and Education Department represent one more attempt to communicate the scientific research of the Acropolis Restoration Service to the wider public. The Department offers a wide range of educational activities addressed to pupils, educators, families and the general public. These activities are based on a set of principles that are in accordance with the concepts of public engagement and Public Archaeology, the field in which the general public becomes aware of and actively involved in the enhancement, protection and conservation of cultural heritage.

These principles are the following:

- An in-depth understanding of the art and history of the Acropolis monuments and a familiarity with the essence of classical antiquity should be accessible by all and not only for the benefit of experts.
- Heritage education, which is the first step towards ensuring the cultivation of respect for the monuments and an interest in their preservation, should begin in early childhood.
- Learning through heritage instead of learning about heritage can help students cultivate their values and develop skills, as well as promote enjoyment and inspiration (Hansen 2014, 8).

It is within this framework that the Acropolis Restoration Service seeks to inform citizens about the importance of public restoration works and, at the same time, to influence positive changes in learning practice. The aim, therefore, is to enhance a cognitive, aesthetic and affective approach to the Acropolis monuments and to promote experiential heritage learning. It is worth noting here that all the learning programmes are provided free of charge and they take place at the archaeological site of the Acropolis in collaboration with the Acropolis Museum.

One of the Department's primary tasks is the organisation of educational programmes for school groups and families, always tailored to the age and the knowledge level of participants (Hadziaslani *et al.* 2018, 850–4). Over the years these programmes have covered a variety of subjects, such as mythology, ancient Greek history, architecture and sculpture of the Acropolis monuments, as well as the contemporary restoration project. Craft or digital workshops conducted as part of these programmes encourage observation, experience, participation and the development of students' creativity. Various activities which allow interaction, sharing, and discussion lead young people to discover, negotiate and construct their sense of participation. Some of the educational programmes of the Department are carried out regularly, while others are implemented in conjunction with temporary exhibitions, anniversaries or special events. Several educational programmes are also held for students on a large scale as open-day programmes.

As there is great demand for participation in all the programmes and the number of the employees in the Department is limited to meet such a need, a large part of the Department's actions were directed towards training school educators, so they can effectively lead the visits and take charge of the learning content. Staff members of the Department (https://www.ysma.gr/en/educational-actions/educational-resources/) then concentrated their efforts in the production of educational resources, both in print and online, in Greek and English. They comprise books, museum trails, museum kits, family back-packs, films and online applications. These resources are also tailored so they can be useful to school groups as well as the general public. They aim at facilitating the dissemination of the learning activities as well as accelerating their impact to a wider audience.

One of the most celebrated activity sets are the museum kits, specially designed for use by groups of students at school (Hadziaslani *et al.* 2011, 52–59). The museum kits can be lent to school groups free of charge and, through them, the museum travels outside of its premises making learning an enjoyable experience. They contain a range of carefully designed materials that can be used according to the teaching style and method of every practitioner. Each kit includes books, games, digital applications, films, models and casts, which can enhance a lesson in the classroom, or in some other place of cultural reference. The museum kits cover eight different topics, which, although separate, they also form part of a standard narrative approaching the culture of ancient Greece holistically.

The second category of resources is the family back-packs and trails available to families visiting the Acropolis site and the Acropolis Museum (https://www.theacropolismuseum.gr/en/content/family-programs). Family back-packs work best when a parent or carer is enabled to support the children's learning during the visit (Gaskins 2008, 11). For this reason it is essential that the adults feel that they have access to adequate resources to answer questions or engage with the exhibits. Most of these resources, which are produced in collaboration with the Acropolis Museum, can be found at the Museum Information Desk and they are offered free of charge. Families can choose between a quick and compact tour using one of the trails, or a longer and more elaborate one, borrowing the back-packs, which are also equipped with games and activities that require families to work together to solve various challenges. Specially designed family labels placed near the exhibits encourage an element of interactivity, increasing the time spent with the display, compared with the traditional text labels. (Hand 2019, 17).

The experience of visiting the site or the museum cannot, of course, be replaced by any digital means, but their use can complement and enhance it. Incorporating digital technologies into heritage learning activities can engage students in ways that traditional learning material cannot. Thus, several online applications have been designed by the Service for educators, students and the general public. It is mainly a series of game-based applications that promote the concept of gamification, which is the use of game elements in a non-game context. This, in turn, automatically becomes more engaging and attains better retention of users (Nechita 2014, 275). These applications can be found on the website of the Acropolis Restoration Service (www.ysma.gr), on the Acropolis Museum website (www.theacropolismuseum.gr) as well as on the Acropolis Educational Resources Repository (http://repository.acropolis-education.gr/acr_edu/). The latter is an online Repository system, developed in collaboration with the Hellenic National Documentation Centre. It incorporates all the Department's educational content, which is navigable by educators, students, families and the wider public, according to their needs and aspirations.

The dialogue between the Department and the educators is also established through special seminars that are held regularly at the Acropolis Museum, as well as throughout Greece and abroad (Kaimara *et al.* 2018, 413–14). These seminars focus on the presentation of the Department's educational resources, on how they can be integrated in school curriculum and on their efficacy during class preparation before a teacher-guided school visit. Moreover, projects that have been implemented by school groups in collaboration with the Department are also presented during these seminars, as a way of inspiring and encouraging educators to carry out their own programmes.

It is therefore evident that, over the last four decades, the Information and Education Department has been active in the field of cultural heritage education by approaching each thematic unit in many different ways, such as the organisation of educational programmes, the creation of educational resources for schools, the implementation of seminars to teachers, the design of trails and games for families and also the creation of web and multimedia educational applications. This holistic approach is driven by the need to improve accessibility, attract audiences of a wide range of ages and backgrounds, maximise the number of participants in the educational activities and also enhance the quality of the visit to the archaeological site or the museum.

A representative case study of such a comprehensive approach that reflects the Department's 'outward-looking' perspective is presented here through the thematic unit of the restoration of the Acropolis Monuments (Kaimara 2015). This topic attracts the interest of the public because it combines ancient world content with technological and scientific advances and their application in archaeology and preservation of heritage monuments. Making this content accessible by the wider public is a challeng-ing and demanding task as it requires the adoption of a broad range of educational strategies and interpretive tools.

The first step in this direction was the organisation of a large-scale educational programme on the Acropolis targeting secondary school students. The programme *Acropolis and Restoration* (Fig. 2.3) was organised for the first time in 1986. Since then, it has been repeated many times aiming to acquaint students with the Acropolis monuments and the importance of their restoration (Kaimara *et al.* 2012). The pres-entation of the works by the specialised personnel of the Service, the *in situ* visit of the students to the Acropolis monuments, as well as their participation in interac-tive workshops and their contact with the various professionals working at the site, offer a multifaceted experience which helps them to understand the importance of the contemporary interventions on ancient monuments. It is an example of the way that public programmes may encourage learning at the archaeological site, providing experiences, addressing participants' multiple aptitudes and promoting discussion and interaction through hands-on activities. At the same time, the staff members can present their work *in situ* and disseminate it to the wider public. Through this process,

Figure 2.3: Educational programme Acropolis and Restoration *(image: T. Souvlakis, 2016, YSMA Archive).*

they actively engage with the young students, feel more empowered and rewarded by their achievements and through their example can inspire a new generation.

The desire to disseminate the programme more widely and multiply its recipients without repeatedly involving a large number of employees has led to the production of a museum kit that can be used by pupils and their teachers for the preparation of their visit to the Acropolis. It is entitled *Restoring the Athenian Acropolis* (https://www.ysma.gr/en/museum-kits/restoring-the-athenian-acropolis/) and aims to teach secondary school students what restoration interventions are currently being undertaken on the Acropolis, why they are being carried out and what methodology is being followed. The kit includes ten educational leaflets divided into two groups together with the film *The Acropolis Restoration Project.* The first group of leaflets presents theoretical issues associated with the restoration of ancient monuments in general and with the Acropolis in particular. One of these leaflets is devoted to suggestions for the use of the educational material for schools through various school subjects. The second group of leaflets gives a detailed presentation of the restoration projects being carried out on each of the Acropolis monuments.

At the same time, thematic seminars on the restoration of the monuments are organized at regular intervals to enhance collaboration with teachers and facilitate their access to an interesting and demanding topic that can be linked to vocational education and pave the way for multilevel discussions with students. These seminars aim at presenting the causes, principles and methodology of the restoration interventions, the completed and current restoration programmes, as well as all the relevant printed, multimedia and online material designed by the Department.

However, as the image of the monuments with the cranes and scaffolding is a topic of discussion for both site and Museum visitors, the next step in opening up to a broader public has been taken with the release of a family trail entitled: *10 Questions About the Restoration of the Acropolis Monuments* (https://www.ysma.gr/en/edu-printed-matters/10-questions-restoration-acropolis-monuments/). Through concise and clear content, the kinds of interventions, the methods of transporting and placing large volumes of marble in their final position in Antiquity, as well as the variety of the specialities of the personnel engaged both in the construction of the monuments and today, in their restoration, are presented. Emphasis is also put on the illustration and graphic design of the printed material, to facilitate understanding, attract interest and cultivate the aesthetics of children and adults.

The most recent and modern medium used for the interpretation of the Acropolis monuments restoration and the development of a meaningful, dynamic and pleasant discourse with the audience is the use of technological advances. By exploiting the full potentiality of new information and communication technologies in the field of heritage education, it is possible to increase people's awareness of the importance attached to the protection of cultural heritage. In this context, *The Glafka Project* (https://theglafkaproject.ysma.gr/), an online application about the Acropolis restoration works has been developed (Kaimara *et al.* 2015). It is a multi-level digital game for both pupils aged 12 years and over and the general public. The leading role belongs to Glafka, a flying owl-robot mascot. The application is based on a scenario combining characters, roles, missions and finally awarding the user for his/her achievements. It aims to familiarise students with the restoration projects of the Acropolis monuments, which are presented through five modules: a) The Journey (damage and reasons for intervention), b) The Help (types of interventions), c) The Crew (the people undertaking the restoration work), d) Action (restoration works that have been carried out on each one of the monuments), and e) In the Future (instruments and new technologies used in the restoration of the Acropolis). Each module includes the preparation, that is a brief presentation of the topic and a test, which is a mini-game. The application is completed with the unit 'Learn More', which includes Glafka's Library for those interested in further information.

During the years, the feedback from evaluations of both the educational programme *Acropolis and Restoration* and the *The Glafka Project* online application has been of decisive importance for their development and improvement. As a result of these evaluations, in the case of the educational programme, the hands-on and interactive character of the workshops has been reinforced, as it seems that they have higher preference rates than the theoretical presentations. Moreover, it became clear that we need to increase the number of involved pupils and expand the audience with the participation of different visitor groups. Similarly, in the case of the online application, the need to adapt it to the requirements of users with learning disabilities, as well as to regularly update its content, providing a reason for the users to return to it, has become apparent.

Conclusions

All the above educational and public engagement activities illustrate the great potential that heritage sites can have as places of learning but, also, as places that promote inspiration, creativity and enjoyment. The Acropolis Restoration Service will continue to creatively exploit the wealth of the Acropolis Monuments, offering the public, ample opportunities to get to know about the monuments and the works carried out on them. It is clear, however, as the experience from the Acropolis projects manifests, that to keep up with a demanding and diversifying audience, professionals are required to explore new presentation techniques continually, utilise new media and reinvent their narrative strategies.

Equally important is the fact that in the long term the documentation of public engagement activities provides an essential archive for monitoring shifts within the discipline of public engagement with the past, in line with the practice of evaluating public programmes across other major European Museums and archaeological sites. At the same time, the Acropolis Restoration Service, through a wide range of educational activities, converts all its experience and expertise on public engagement into practice.

Based on this remarkable legacy, YSMA aims at harmonising with the multilevel demands and challenges of demanding and rapidly shifting audiences, through synergies with various agencies. In this way, the heritage content will be publicly available to the maximum and a new generation of more responsible citizens, members of a more inclusive and informed society will be built up.

References

Alexopoulos, Y. (2012) Η τεκμηρίωση του έργου της αποκατάστασης του Ερεχθείου και η ηλεκτρονική διαχείρισή της. In F. Mallouchou-Tufano, Ch. Bouras & A. Papanikolaou (eds), *Η αποκατάσταση του Ερεχθείου (1979-1987)*, 621–8. Athens, ΥΣΜΑ.

Alexopoulos, Y. & Katsianis, M. (2012) Digital applications for projecting the Acropolis restoration works on the internet. *The Acropolis Restoration News* 12, 20–3.

Eleftheriou,V. & Lempidaki, E. (2016) Ψηφιακές εφαρμογές διαχείρισης πολιτιστικού περιεχομένου στα αναστηλωτικά έργα της Ακρόπολης. In K. Skriapas & A. Demeslis (eds), *1ο Πανελλήνιο Συνέδριο Ψηφιοποίησης Πολιτιστικής Κληρονομιάς, Βόλος, 24-26 Σεπτεμβρίου 2015, Πρακτικά*, 526–31. Βόλος, Δίκτυο Περραιβία.

Gaskins, S. (2008) Designing exhibitions to support families' cultural understandings. *Exhibitionist* 27 (1), 11–19.

Hand, C. (2019) *Engaging Visitors in Natural History Museums. A NEMO - The Learning Museum Group Report*. Berlin, Network of European Museum Organisations.

Hansen, A. (2014) The heritage learning framework and the Heritage Learning Outcomes. In D. Christidou (ed.), *Implementing Heritage Learning Outcomes*, 7–24. Östersund, Jamtli.

Hadziaslani, K., Kaimara, E. & Leonti, A. (2011) *Ακρόπολη και Εκπαίδευση*. Athens, ΥΣΜΑ.

Hadziaslani, K., Kaimara, E. & Leonti, A. (2018) Εκπαιδευτικές δράσεις του Τομέα Ενημέρωσης κι Εκπαίδευσης (2003-2013). In Ch. Bouras & V. Eleftheriou (eds), *Επεμβάσεις στα μνημεία της Ακρόπολης 2000-2012. Τα ολοκληρωμένα προγράμματα, τόμος* III, 850–71. Athens, ΥΣΜΑ.

Kaimara, I. (2015) Η Αναστήλωση της Ακρόπολης για παιδιά... στον Βράχο και στο διαδίκτυο. In Ch. Bouras & V. Eleftheriou (eds), *6η Διεθνής Συνάντηση για την Αποκατάσταση των Μνημείων Ακροπόλεως, Πρακτικά*, Αθήνα 4-5 Οκτωβρίου 2013, 270–81. Athens, ΥΣΜΑ.

Kaimara, I., Leonti, A. & Paraschou, S. (2018) Μεθοδολογία ενίσχυσης της αυτόνομης σχολικής και οικογενειακής επίσκεψης στον αρχαιολογικό χώρο και στο Μουσείο Ακρόπολης. In M. Korres & V. Eleftheriou (eds), *Ειδικά θέματα έρευνας και εφαρμογών στα αναστηλωτικά έργα της Ακρόπολης την περίοδο 2010-2015, Πρακτικά*, Αθήνα 18-19 Νοεμβρίου 2016, 413–24. Athens, ΥΣΜΑ.

Kaimara, I., Leonti, A., Paraschou, S. & Hadziaslani, C. (2012) Educational programme 'A Day at the Acropolis restoring its monuments'. *The Acropolis Restoration News* 12, 24–9.

Kaimara, I., Leonti, A., Paraschou, S. & Hadziaslani, C. (2015) 'The Glafka Project': presentation and evaluation of an online educational application for the restoration of the Acropolis monuments. *The Acropolis Restoration News* 14–15, 33–7.

Katsianis, M. (2013) Current challenges in documenting the restoration works on the Acropolis of Athens. *The Acropolis Restoration News* 13, 22–5.

Katsianis, M. & Kamatsos, P. (2016) The digital repository of YSMA: Contribution to the preservation of the collective memory of the restoration interventions. *The Acropolis Restoration News* 16, 22–6.

Lempidaki, E. (2015) Η τεκμηρίωση των αναστηλωτικών έργων στην Ακρόπολη και η ψηφιακή της διαχείριση. In Ch. Bouras & V. Eleftheriou (eds), *6η Διεθνής Συνάντηση για την Αποκατάσταση των Μνημείων Ακροπόλεως, Πρακτικά*, Αθήνα 4-5 Οκτωβρίου 2013, 216–31. Athens, ΥΣΜΑ.

Lempidaki, E., Karakitsou, E., Petropoulou, E. & Alexopoulos, Y. (2018) Η ψηφιακή διαχείριση της τεκμηρίωσης στα αναστηλωτικά έργα της Ακρόπολης (2000–2012). In Ch. Bouras & V. Eleftheriou (eds) *Επεμβάσεις στα μνημεία της Ακρόπολης 2000-2012. Τα ολοκληρωμένα προγράμματα, τόμος* III, 812–47. Athens, ΥΣΜΑ.

Mallouchou-Tufano, F. (1992) Documentation of the restoration project for the Acropolis monuments. Creation of a data bank. In J. Boardman & D. Kurtz (eds), *Data and Image Processing in Classical Archaeology, Ravello, 3-4 April, Proceedings,* 21–22. Firenze, Edizioni All'Insegna del Giglio.

Mallouchou-Tufano, F. & Alexopoulos, Y. (2007) Digital management of the documentation of the Acropolis restoration. In *AntiCIPAting the Future of the Cultural Past XXI CIPA Conference, Athens, 1-6 October 2007,* 475–9. Athens, CIPA.

Mallouchou-Tufano, F. & Bouras, Ch. (eds) (2012) *Α. Παπανικολάου, Η αποκατάσταση του Ερεχθείου (1979-1987).* Athens, ΥΣΜΑ.

Mallouchou-Tufano, F., Alexopoulos, Y. & Guimier-Sorbets, A. M. (1990) Conservation des monuments de l' Acropole: le traitement de la documentation. *Bulletin de Recherches sur l' Information en Sciences Économiques, Humaines et Sociales* 15(92), 86–8.

Mallouchou-Tufano, F., Alexopoulos, Y. & Lempidaki, E. (2003) Η ηλεκτρονική διαχείριση της τεκμηρίωσης των αναστηλωτικών έργων Ακροπόλεως στα εργοτάξια των μνημείων. In F. Mallouchou-Tufano (ed.), *5η Διεθνής Συνάντηση για την Αποκατάσταση των Μνημείων Ακροπόλεως, Αθήνα 4-6 Οκτωβρίου 2002, Πρακτικά,* 353–62. Athens, ΕΣΜΑ.

Mavromati, D., (2015) Τοπογραφικές και φωτογραμμετρικές αποτυπώσεις στην Ακρόπολη των Αθηνών. In Ch. Bouras & V. Eleftheriou (eds) *6η Διεθνής Συνάντηση για την Αποκατάσταση των Μνημείων Ακροπόλεως, Πρακτικά, Αθήνα 4-5 Οκτωβρίου 2013,* 233–48. Athens, ΥΣΜΑ.

Nechita, F. (2014) The new concepts shaping the marketing communication strategies of museums. *Bulletin of the Transylvania University of Brasov* 7(56.1), 269–78.

Petropoulou, E. & Koutsadelis, K. (2018) Η ανασύνθεση της πρόσφατης ιστορίας των αρχιτεκτονικών μελών των Προπυλαίων μέσω της ηλεκτρονικής Βάσης Δεδομένων της ΥΣΜΑ. In M. Korres & V. Eleftheriou (eds), *Ειδικά θέματα έρευνας και εφαρμογών στα αναστηλωτικά έργα της Ακρόπολης την περίοδο 2010-2015, Πρακτικά, Αθήνα 18-19 Νοεμβρίου 2016,* 401–12. Athens, ΥΣΜΑ.

The Venice Charter (1964) ICOMOS, International Charter for the Conservation and Restoration of Monuments and Sites. *2nd International Congress of Architects and Technicians of Historic Monuments, article 16,* Venice, ICOMOS.

Chapter 3

The New Concept of the Berlin Museum für Vor- und Frühgeschichte – Archaeology in a Historically-engaged Museum Building

Marion Bertram

The collection of the Museum für Vor- und Frühgeschichte (Museum of Prehistory and Early History) goes back to the Cabinet of Curiosities of the Prussian Kings. The prehistoric antiquities have been part of the Staatliche Museen zu Berlin (Berlin State Museums), formerly known as Royal Museums, since 1829. The Museum's frequent relocations are part of its eventful history. Since 1837, the exhibition has been shown at six different sites (Menghin 2004–2005). After the Second World War the collection was divided between the Museum of Prehistory and Early History in West Berlin, housed in the Langhansbau of the Charlottenburg Palace from 1960 onwards, and the Museum Island in East Berlin, where exhibitions were shown in the Pergamon Museum from 1963 and, later, in the Bode Museum. After the reunification of Germany, the collection was reunited in the Langhansbau of the Charlottenburg Palace in 1992, before moving to its former home, the Neues Museum (New Museum) on the Museum Island in 2009.

The Museum's framework for both research and exhibitions is the comparative archaeology of Old Europe and adjacent regions. In addition, the museum covers the archaeology of Berlin, as the Director of the museum is also the county archaeologist. The current collection encompasses 350,000 objects from the Palaeolithic to the High Middle Ages, from all parts of Europe, the entire Mediterranean region, North Africa, as well as the Near and Far East. As the result of ongoing excavations in Berlin an increasing number of post-medieval finds are now part of the museum's collection, some of them dating to the most recent past.

Since 2009, the Museum für Vor- und Frühgeschichte has exhibited its rich collections on the Museum Island in the Neues Museum. The British architect David Chipperfield was commissioned with planning the rebuilding of the war ruins in 1997. The reconstruction and restoration of the museum took place between 2003 and 2009.

The current exhibition and the Museum's public engagement strategy can only be understood against the backdrop of the museum's history. Therefore, it makes sense to give a summary of the educational concepts of the mid-19th century.

The Altes Museum (Old Museum) built by Karl Friedrich Schinkel at the Lustgarten (Pleasure Garden) opened in 1830 and was Berlin's first purpose-built museum (Vogtherr 1997). It was meant for the enjoyment of the 'High Arts', in those times meaning mainly art pieces of classical Greek and Roman antiquity. Plans for a second museum were drawn up shortly afterwards (van Wezel 2003). Construction of the Neues Museum commenced in 1843 according to plans by Friedrich August Stüler. The concept of the new museum lay in educating visitors about history. The elaborate interior design, as well as the decoration of the exhibition rooms, matched the contents and promoted the understanding of the exhibits (Bertram 2004–2005; Blauert & Bähr 2012).

The cultural history of humankind was descriptively portrayed ascending from the ground floor to the top, starting with the very beginnings and ending with the 19th century. The ground floor was therefore reserved for the so-called 'primitive cultures', encompassing in those days the prehistoric, Egyptian and ethnographic collections. Illustrating the spirit of the time, the exquisite first floor was reserved for the expansive collection of plaster casts, copying the most famous works of classical antiquity, the High Middle Ages and the Renaissance. The second floor was used for exhibiting arts and crafts collections as well as the Kupferstichkabinett (Prints Cabinet). Due to numerous moves and changes, the original concept began to disintegrate from the 1880s onwards.

The Vaterländische Saal (National Room), was the first purpose-built exhibition room for a prehistoric collection in Europe. The paintings on the top part of the walls were particularly innovative for that time. The pictures of northern mythology are the first of their kind and the southern wall was illustrated with the first pictorial representation of the so-called Three Age System (Stone Age, Bronze Age, Iron Age), showing weapons, vessels and jewellery from the prehistoric collection (Fig. 3.1) (Bertram 2011).

Due to a lack of space, the prehistoric collection was moved to the Völkerkundemuseum (Museum of Ethnology) (Gärtner 2004–2005). After the move and until the Second World War, the Vaterländische Saal was used for medieval German sculptures and later for Egyptian antiquities. The Neues Museum was extensively damaged during the war and the building ruins were left exposed to the elements for many decades.

Although the GDR finally began planning the rebuilding of the Neues Museum in the 1980s, the plans were stopped after reunification. As part of comprehensive talks regarding the future of the recently reunited Berlin State Museums it was decided that all archaeological collections should be exhibited in one location, namely on the Museum Island. The Egyptian Museum, as well as the Museum of Prehistory and Early History, were to move back into the Neues Museum.

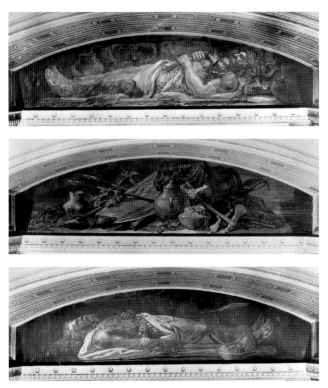

Figure 3.1: Vaterländischer Saal (National Room): Lunette paintings on the south wall depicting the so-called Three Ages System (Stone Age–Bronze Age–Iron Age) (image: © Staatliche Museen zu Berlin, Museum für Vor- und Frühgeschichte, photographed in 1919).

David Chipperfield was successful in restoring the ruins carefully, supplementing destroyed architectural features without completely rebuilding them (Staatliche Museen zu Berlin 2009). The building does not shy away from showing its wounds, making it possible to read its history. In this way, the building itself is part of the dialogue between the public, the collections and the history of the Museum itself. The careful, almost archaeological, restoration is a matching backdrop for the archaeological exhibits standing in constant dialogue with each other. Each room has its very own history, dimension and form. The exhibition design was tailored to take these multi-layered dimensions into account. Material and proportions of display cases and other elements of the exhibition correspond with the historical and modern interior design.

The current spatial concept of the Neues Museum is based partly on the historical uses of the rooms, and partly on practical considerations (Wemhoff 2015; Seyfried & Wemhoff 2016). Level 0 and the newly built rooms in the north-western part of the building are being used for the heavy Egyptian objects for structural reasons. Level 3, on the other hand, is particularly suitable for exhibiting the numerous smaller artefacts of the Museum of Prehistory and Early History. The main historical room of the Egyptian collection, the Mythologische Saal (Mythological Room) is situated in the north wing of the ground floor, now known as level 1. The Vaterländische Saal, designed initially to hold the prehistoric collection, is in the south wing of the same level. Directly above the Vaterländische Saal, on Level 2, lies the Römische Saal (Roman Room). Its history and design made it particularly suitable for exhibiting artefacts from the Roman provinces. The corner pillars were integrated into the new spatial concept.

On Level 0, one can see the thematic rooms of the Egyptian collection. On Levels 1 and 2, the south wings are occupied by the Museum of Prehistory and Early History and the north wings by the Egyptian Museum. Level 3 shows a chronological exhibition of European prehistory. The new permanent exhibition of the Museum of Prehistory and Early History was opened in two stages in 2009 and 2014.

The Museum of Prehistory and Early History exhibits more than 6000 of its objects in 15 rooms using a total of 3540 m². The tour starts on Level 1 in the Vaterländische Saal, whose history has already been described. It seemed obvious to use this historically significant room as a starting point. In order to preserve the historical impression of the room the inventory was kept unobtrusive. The history of the museum is documented by using four double display cabinets. Symbolic finds testify to the development of the collection and the concept of its presentation. The pictorial representations of Nordic mythology are made accessible through historical photographs and short textual descriptions about the different scenes. Finally, three display cases are used to display the original finds depicted in the paintings of the Three Age System.

The next two rooms compare the history of two regions from the Early Bronze Age to the classical Greek and Roman period using Schliemann's collection of Trojan antiquities and the Cyprus collection. Only a small but representative proportion from Troy, once numbering 10,000 objects and coming from all layers of this unique site, can be exhibited.

The current Cyprus Room is one of the rooms which were destroyed quite heavily during the Second World War. The large double display cases between the pillars and the tall wall display cases take into account the state of the room and its architectural arrangement. The objects shown in this room originate from the Antiquities Collection and the Museum of Prehistory and Early History.

The tour on Level 1 initially passes through the rooms of the Egyptian Museum. Nefertiti is looking across the enfilade from the Nordkuppelraum (Northern Cupola Room) at the Roman colossal statue of Helios from Egypt dominating the Südkuppelraum (Southern Cupola Room). The reference points 'Sun' and 'Egypt' form a wonderful connection in this setup, which is interrupted by another highlight half-way, namely the 'Xanten Boy' from the Antiquities Collection. At this point, in the Bacchus-Saal (Bacchus Room), begins the archaeology of the Roman provinces. From 2009 onwards the 'Xanten Boy' has been positioned on a flat pedestal for the first time. This means that the visitors come across the statue, which was once used as a dumb waiter in the same manner as the Romans came across it at a banquet.

The next room is the Römische Saal, once the home of cast plaster copies of famous Roman statues. Views of 17 Roman towns once decorated the walls. Today most of the decorations have been lost. The historical arrangement offers a suitable setting for the archaeology of the Roman provinces, covering the themes military, production, trade, everyday life, games and burial (Fig. 3.2). The Südkuppelraum exhibits objects linked to cult and gods. The historical structure of the room was completely destroyed. David Chipperfield managed to design an ingenious new solution using the historical tiles.

It seemed apposite to introduce Rome's northern neighbours in the following room. The presentation of Germanic culture is based on different cultural areas.

Figure 3.2: Detail of the Roman Room (image: © Staatliche Museen zu Berlin, Museum für Vor- und Frühgeschichte, photo: A. Kleuker, 2009).

Each display case exhibits finds from different regional groups: the so-called North Sea Germans, the Rhine-Weser, Elb and the Eastern Germans. The famous elite burial of Lübsow, as well as other Roman imports from German sites shown in the exhibition, belong to the Antiquities Collection. Busts of Roman emperors and Roman depictions of 'barbarians' make for a particularly interesting interplay. A side room provides the opportunity to engage visitors with the museum's history. Fragments from destroyed building elements which were recovered from the rubble are displayed on the walls and in the original display cases from initial fittings of the museum.

The tour continues into a large room where the archaeology of the Migration Period and the Middle Ages is displayed. Besides numerous objects from the Museum of Prehistory and Early History, exhibits from other collections of the Museum Island are also displayed, including the Antiquities Collection, the Numismatic Cabinet, the Museum of Byzantine Art and the Sculpture Collection. It is a considerable challenge to cover the entire time span from late Antiquity to the European Middle Ages in one room. It is unlikely that visitors will grasp the complex dimensions of social and cultural change after just one visit to the museum. In addition to the written explanations in the exhibition there are specialised guided tours and publications.

Although most objects are exhibited inside display cases some larger items are positioned in the room by themselves. The exhibits include gold jewellery and prestige weapons of the migration period, coins of early medieval rulers, Merovingian grave goods, Byzantine jewellery as well as finds from the Avares, Slavs, Vikings and Balts. Freestanding exhibits include a chancel screen from the old St Peter's Basilica in Rome and a stele with a silver denarius depicting Charlemagne. He probably commissioned this coin in the classical style shortly after he was crowned emperor in Rome. The copy of the so-called 'Door of Paradise' from the Baptistery of Florence Cathedral reminds visitors of the historical use of this room for displaying casts of famous art pieces from the Renaissance. Laminated texts inform visitors about the significance of the different scenes.

Visitors can reach Level 3 via the large central staircase. This floor only reopened in June 2014 with a reworked permanent exhibition. The prehistory of Europe is presented using more than 1500 m², covering the period from the Old Stone Age to the Pre-Roman Iron Age. To begin with, however, the visitor is led back to the history of the Neues Museum and Prehistoric Collection. The first point of contact was the fact that the Rote Saal (Red Room), was formerly used to house the teaching collection of the Prints Cabinet. The bust of Albrecht Dürer bears witness to the museum's history. The rediscovery of a collection of historical display cases with intact interior fittings was an additional reason for the detour into the museum's history. Old documents prove that the display cases were used for the prehistoric exhibits in the late 19th century. Using the old display cases, the room was recreated in the style of a 19th-century teaching collection. The theme of this room is the historical collection which formed the basis for the current Museum of Prehistory and Early History in the 19th and early 20th century.

The next room, showing recent archaeological finds from Berlin, stands in stark contrast to the Rote Saal both in terms of architecture and content. We are now in the north-western part of the museum and its side rooms which were completely destroyed during the Second World War. A single large display case is used to exhibit recent finds from medieval and post-medieval excavations from the city centre of Berlin. A city map animation illustrates the development of the 'double-city' Berlin-Cölln.

It is at this point that the tour of the prehistory of Europe begins (Fig. 3.3). The large modern hall allowed a free placement of the exhibition elements. Large platforms with integrated low display cases enable extensive descriptions and explanations. This lower level is combined with tall display cases which are used to portray Palaeolithic and Neolithic cultural groups and their typical tools, weapons, jewellery and vessels. The Neanderthal skull from Le Moustier in France is one of the most famous objects of this collection. The face of the 11-year-old boy was reconstructed for the new exhibition using the original skull. A media station can be used to obtain more detailed information about the discovery and recent scientific research results on this human skull. Larger media stations illustrate the large upheavals of the Stone Age: the evolution of mankind and the neolithisation of Europe.

At first glance, the following Bronze Age room looks like a procession route leading to the famous Berlin Gold Hat. The Gold Hat has its dedicated room. Upon closer observation, however, visitors discover a comprehensive and wide-ranging picture of Bronze Age society and culture in Europe. The elaborate diagrams on the front of the display cases are followed by in-depth explanations on the back of the cases. Some cases include integrated media stations which inform in more detail

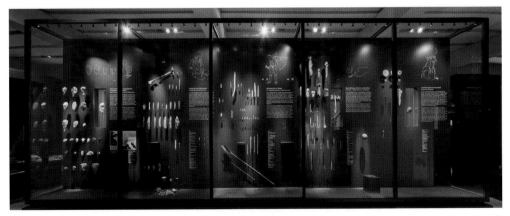

Figure 3.3: Detail of the Stone Age Room (image: © 16elements GmbH/museumstechnik GmbH., 2014).

about significant excavations. The themes are metal extraction and production, symbols of power and identity and trade and communication. Within these themes, regional differences between Bronze Age cultures in Europe and the Mediterranean are compared.

The Bronze Age exhibits also include objects from the rich inventory of the Antiquities Collection. Furthermore, the collaboration with the county archaeology office of Mecklenburg-Vorpommern enabled the presentation of a spectacular find. A recent excavation in the Tollense Valley uncovered the oldest battlefield to date in Europe. After collecting 3D data it was possible to exhibit a 3D print of a section of the burial site for the first time as part of the exhibition on the Bronze Age.

The Berlin Gold Hat is the most famous exhibit in the Neues Museum apart from Nefertiti. The Gold Hat is, just like Nefertiti, exhibited in its own room, providing in-depth information about the symbols displayed on it, as well as on the astronomical and calendrical knowledge of the Bronze Age. A circular console combines descriptive texts with diagrams and integrated display cases, enhancing the narrative.

The next room was destined to be at the heart of the educational activities. After a competition for ideas as to the design of the room, which included many interesting interactive proposals on the topic of 'Mankind and Environment in Prehistoric Times', the room was turned out as an educational hub in time for the opening in 2014. The central installation in this room is called the 'time machine'. In this room visitors learn how archaeologists study the excavated finds, and how they use material culture to reconstruct prehistoric communities. We use several old dioramas to enable a retrospective of museum learning practices from the 1960s to today. The main attraction, however, is a new documentary which can also be used interactively via a control console. A significant number of curators and learning specialists collaborated over the production of this film, creating 'landscape narratives', illustrating the history of a lakeside and its changing inhabitants through time. The audience can engage by recognising many objects from the Museum's display in this film, including tools, weapons, jewellery and vessels. Visitors can then learn how the objects were used and worn in context.

Modern computer animation methods enable this as well as the creation of impressive time-lapse sequences of watercolour paintings, representing different stages of the timeline. At the same time, a narrator tells a story for each different scene. The film and timeline have been evaluated with regards to audience engagement and the results have shown that different age groups engage very well with its content.

The final room covering the Pre-Roman Iron Age is equally charged with high educational content. The opening theme of this room is the extraction and production of iron. Results from recent excavations carried out around Berlin are presented and expanded on in a media station. The comparative presentation of Iron Age groups encompasses the Lusatian culture, the Pomeranian and House Urns cultures, the

Hallstatt culture, the Celtic La Tène culture, the Germanic Jastorf culture and the Scythians. This room also provides the opportunity to engage the public with the challenging topic of previous historic and archaeological interpretations: this is achieved through the example of the site La Tène, raising questions about the interpretation of the finds in the mid-19th century. Moreover, Roman finds from the Germanic and Celtic areas dating to the 1st century BC demonstrate the growing power of the Roman Empire north of the Alps.

In conclusion, it is possible to say that the Neues Museum has implemented 'traditional' methods of display while at the same time employing the rich history of the building in its efforts to engage its new audiences. However, within the building, there are different approaches. The Egyptian Museum regarded itself, at the time of the opening in 2009, more as an art museum, therefore only offering descriptive texts on walls and object descriptions, while a decision was made against the use of media stations. The rooms used by the Museum of Prehistory and Early History provide content via information boards, descriptive texts, diagrams and maps within display cases and extended object narratives. In addition, the entire museum is supplemented using free audio guides in various languages. The audio guide expands on the details about the museum's history and architecture and the exhibition content. Free leaflets on topics extending the exhibition's narratives and other contextual information are also available.

The reconstructed Neues Museum has won numerous significant architectural prizes. The fascination about the building as well as the respect for it as a historic monument played a major role while planning the exhibition halls and displays. It is, however, not possible to design and implement the presentation of a collection in a building like the Neues Museum without making compromises and restraining our ambitions. Today the Neues Museum attracts a very diverse and multicultural audience and is proud to present to the visitors its unique 'ensemble' of diachronic collections and their history as well as the history of interpretations, while reconciling with the monument's and the city's unique recent historical past.

References

Bertram, M. (2004–2005) Vom „Museum Vaterländischer Alterthümer" im Schloss Monbijou zur „Sammlung der Nordischen Alterthümer" im Neuen Museum. Die Ära Ledebur 1829–1873. In W. Menghin (ed.), *Das Berliner Museum für Vor- und Frühgeschichte*, 31–79. *Festschrift zum 175-jährigen Bestehen*. Berlin, Acta Praehistoria et Archaeologica 36/37.

Bertram, M. (2011) Die Konzeption der Sammlung Vaterländischer Altertümer im Neuen Museum. In E. Bergvelt, D. J. Meijers, L. Tibbe & E. van Wezel (eds), *Museale Spezialisierung und Nationalisierung ab 1830*, 91–104. Berlin, Berliner Schriften zur Museumsforschung 29.

Blauert, E. & Bähr A. (eds) (2012) *Neues Museum. Architecture, Collections, History*. Berlin, Nicolai.

Gärtner, T. (2004–2005) Begründer einer international vergleichenden Forschung – Adolf Bastian und Albert Voß (1874–1906). In W. Menghin (ed.), *Das Berliner Museum für Vor- und Frühgeschichte. Festschrift zum 175-jährigen Bestehen*, 80–102. Berlin, Acta Praehistorica et Archaeologica 36/37.

Menghin, W. (ed.) (2004–2005) *Das Berliner Museum für Vor- und Frühgeschichte. Festschrift zum 175-jährigen Bestehen.* Berlin, Acta Praehistorica et Archaeologica 36/37.

Staatliche Museen zu Berlin (eds) (2009) *Das Neue Museum Berlin. Konservieren, Restaurieren, Weiterbauen im Welterbe.* Leipzig, E. A. Seemann.

Seyfried, F. & Wemhoff, M. (eds) (2016) *Neues Museum Berlin. Egyptian Museum and Papyrus Collection, Museum of Prehistory and Early History.* München, Prestel.

Vogtherr, C. M. (1997) *Das Königliche Museum zu Berlin. Planungen und Konzeption des ersten Berliner Kunstmuseums.* Berlin, Beiheft zum Jahrbuch der Berliner Museen 39.

Wemhoff, M. (ed.) (2015) *Zwischen Neandertaler und Berolina. Archäologische Schätze im Neuen Museum.* Regensburg, *Die Sammlungen des Museums für Vor- und Frühgeschichte 3.*

Wezel, E. van (2003) *Die Konzeptionen des Alten und Neuen Museums zu Berlin und das sich wandelnde historische Bewusstsein.* Berlin, Beiheft zum Jahrbuch der Berliner Museen 41.

Chapter 4

'Isn't There an App for That Yet?' Evaluating the 'Wall of Cambridge' iPad App as a Means of Public Engagement

Jody Joy and Sarah-Jane Harknett

The so-called 'Cambridge Wall' (Fig. 4.1) is one of the most prominent displays at the Museum of Archaeology and Anthropology (MAA), Cambridge. It comprises three connected cases and is a complicated display intended to work on two levels to show archaeological stratigraphy and geographical location. It is popular with visitors but, because of the density of the displays, there are no object labels. Various surveys indicated that many visitors found this frustrating because they understandably wanted to discover more about the objects on display. To help solve this issue, an iPad app providing more detailed information about individual objects was developed in 2014. A complementary hand-list was also offered to cater to those visitors less comfortable with digital technology.

In this paper, we evaluate the success of the app and the hand-list as means of public engagement by drawing on evaluations of museum visitors, as well as download statistics and user information provided by the Apple App Store software. We conclude with a comparative assessment of digital and analogue resources as means of museum engagement.

The 'Cambridge Wall'

Originally founded in 1883, MAA has been in its present location on Downing Street, Cambridge since 1913 (Elliott & Thomas 2011, 6). The museum holds around 1 million artefacts ranging from 1.8 million-year-old stone tools to contemporary artworks. In comparison to the size of the collections, the display space is limited and comprises just three permanent galleries. MAA is one of eight University of Cambridge Museums and collections and has long been a base for teaching and research (Smith 2009). Still, it is also a public institution and currently attracts 80,000 visitors per year. The museum appeals to the many international visitors to the city, as well as people living in Cambridge and the surrounding region (Harknett 2013; 2016).

As part of an initiative to increase accessibility, a major redevelopment was completed in 2012. In addition to a new front door and the creation of a shop and temporary exhibition space, the Cambridge Gallery was refurbished. The new display was conceived around the local archaeology collection, primarily collected by the Cambridge Antiquarian Society (Elliott & Thomas 2011, 6). It introduces the archaeology of the region and a particular challenge was to make it exciting and relevant to both local and international audiences. Innovative displays were created, including the Cambridge Wall, which occupies a prominent location in the gallery (Fig. 4.1). The 'wall' contains over 150 objects displayed in three layers of perspex, each representing a different period: medieval, Roman and prehistoric. The prehistoric objects are displayed at the back because they are the furthest away in time, with the Roman objects in the middle and medieval towards the front. A map overlay on the outside of the case shows the locations where the objects were found, and the backboard shows the local geology. There are no object labels in the case; a single text panel at the bottom explains its layout.

In response to visitor demand, a hand-list of the objects was created in 2013. This is available in the gallery, with multiple copies located on top of a nearby case. An app, created by a local company Atlas Live and funded by a grant from Arts Council England via the University of Cambridge Museums Major Partner Museum Programme, obtained by a former colleague, Dr Chris Wingfield, was made available in the gallery from 2013 via an iPad offered on request from museum staff. It was launched for free download on the Apple website in October 2014 (http://maa.cam.ac.uk/category/collections-2/ipad-app/).

Figure 4.1: The Cambridge Wall display (image: © Museum of Archaeology and Anthropology, 2014).

Both resources provide basic data for each object on display, including broad chronological period, findspot and museum accession number. In addition, the app begins with an instruction screen. In recognition of its availability online and its potential use outside of the museum, it also contains front-facing features such as a screen showing 360° views of each of the three museum galleries, a visit-us screen and a page allowing users to sign up to our museum newsletter and friends page. To recreate the Cambridge Wall, a digital impression of the find locations was first created. Images of each of the objects were then placed overlaying this basic map, each in the exact location and orientation as they appear in the display. As the end result was visually quite dense, filters were added to recreate the prehistoric, Roman and medieval layers visible in the display (Fig. 4.2). It is also possible to select individual objects and access basic information about them (Fig. 4.3).

Alternative map and satellite views were also created. This feature was aimed at users accessing the app outside the gallery so they could identify and access information about objects found in particular areas. Audio clips for eight objects were also created. These were intended to provide further information about selected objects but were also scripted to create links with, and send visitors to, other objects on display elsewhere in the gallery.

Evaluation of the App Based on Downloads

We conducted an evaluation based on download and usage statistics three months after the app was first made available for download (Table 4.1). As of 5 January 2015 it was downloaded 104 times. After a relatively slow start, there was a peak in activity during

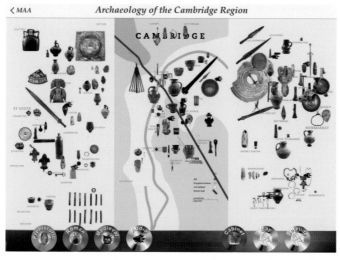

Figure 4.2: Representation of the Cambridge Wall as it appears on the app (image: © Museum of Archaeology and Anthropology, 2014).

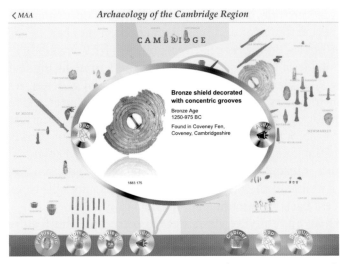

Figure 4.3: Object information as it is presented by the app (image: © Museum of Archaeology and Anthropology, 2014).

Table 4.1: Cumulative downloads and individual user sessions per week

Week	Downloads	Sessions
9/9/14	8	9
06/10/14	16	20
13/10/14	24	32
20/10/14	36	57
27/10/14	48	83
03/11/14	53	108
10/11/14	59	124
17/11/14	60	138
24/11/14	68	178
01/12/14	70	195
08/12/14	80	221
15/12/14	88	238
22/12/14	93	253
29/12/14	98	270
05/01/15	104	278

November. This corresponded well with a period when the profile of the app was raised, particularly during a festival celebrating Cambridge University Museums called 'Curating Cambridge', which ran from 20 October–23 November 2014. Overall, there was a steady number of downloads (5–10 downloads and ten or so users per week) throughout the evaluation. Particularly striking was the number of individual sessions during late October and late November. For example, the week ending 24 November saw only eight new downloads and use by 12 users, but there were 40 user sessions. This may reflect heavy use by one or two individuals, but the reasons for this are not obvious. Unfortunately, the available statistics did not allow us to investigate this further.

These data also allowed assessment of how long the app was used for (Table 4.2). They showed that for the vast majority of sessions (179), users spent less than 1 minute accessing the app, and only five sessions lasted 30 minutes or more. This was disappointing and prompted further investigation to establish why users seemed to be relatively poorly engaged by the app (see below).

More impressive was its potential international reach. Although we cannot be certain which countries it was accessed from, in the first three months the app was

Table 4.2: Duration of use

Duration (minutes)	Sessions
1	179
2	20
3	18
4	16
5	13
10	20
20	7
30	1
Longer	4

Table 4.3: Frequency each screen was accessed

Screen	Views
Cambridge Wall	283
Friends	88
Galleries	250
Home	947
Introduction screen	170
Timeline	246
Visit us	89

available it was downloaded and accessed by users whose iPad default language settings were set to more than 30 different languages. This perhaps should not be surprising, given that there are many international visitors to the museum. In addition, numerous people living in Cambridge and the region may not have English as their first language. Many of these individuals also may have downloaded the app from abroad, but unfortunately, we have no way of quantifying this.

The statistics also allowed us to analyse how the app was used, providing the number of times individual screens were viewed (Table 4.3). Unfortunately, these data are limited as we cannot link numbers to individual users. For example, did all of the 104 users visit the Timeline screen, or did a smaller number of users access it on multiple occasions? Presumably, most users accessed the Cambridge Wall, Gallery and Timeline screens, but we cannot be certain. Unsurprisingly, because of the way the app is navigated where the Home Screen acts as the anchor point, this was accessed most often (947 times), followed by the Cambridge Wall (283), Galleries (250) and Timeline (246) screens. The Visit-Us (89) and Museum Friends (88) screens were understandably accessed fewer times.

Summary and Further Questions

The usage and download statistics for the first three months were relatively modest. This was probably partly because we had no budget to publicise the app. We promoted it through posters, social media and at museum events but, in hindsight, we should have considered this more fully. We concentrated too much on making the app work well, but if no one knows about it that effort may be wasted. The budget for the development and creation of the app was around £10,000. With only 100 downloads in the first three months it means the initial cost to download ratio was quite high but this can only improve as more individuals download it. The ratio also looks much more cost-effective when we consider the cost to user ratio instead. Of more concern to us than the low number of downloads was that the majority of users appeared to access the app for less than 1 minute. The numbers may also be affected because the app is currently only available for the iPad. Developing an equivalent app for the iPhone and Android devices could help improve these numbers. But mobile phones can be limiting because their small size creates barriers in terms of engagement and informal learning between individuals (Fisher & Moses 2013, 3).

Table 4.4: Age distribution of respondents

Age	App	Hardcopy	Total	Percentage
Under 17	2	2	4	5
18–24	8	7	15	20
25–34	9	6	15	20
35–49	10	7	17	23
50–64	8	9	17	23
65+	2	5	7	9
Total	39	36	75	

Table 4.5: Location of residence of respondents

	App	Hardcopy	Total	Percentage
Cambridge City	6	6	12	16
Cambridgeshire	7	5	12	16
Elsewhere in the UK	8	9	17	23
Cambridge University student	4	7	11	14
Visitor from overseas	14	9	23	31
Total	39	36	75	

Evaluation of Resources in the Museum

Over the summer and autumn of 2015 a second evaluation was undertaken focusing on the use of the two resources in the Clarke Gallery and a small team of volunteers was trained in suitable evaluation techniques. Thirty-nine visitors were interviewed about the app and 36 concerning the hand-list (Harknett 2016). First, a visitor was approached and asked to take part in the study. If they agreed, they were then supplied with either the hardcopy hand-list or an iPad with the app. The evaluator timed how long the visitor engaged with the resource and noted how they used it in conjunction with the Cambridge Wall display. Once the visitor had explored the resource they were interviewed about their experience. The hand-list was used as a useful comparator, providing an analogue alternative to digital technology. For easy comparison, the same questions were used for both the app and hand-list. Tables 4.4 and 4.5 provide age, distribution, sex and the location of residence of the respondents. Only 23% of the visitors recorded using the two resources had visited the Museum of Archaeology and Anthropology before.

The average time spent using the app in the gallery was 5 minutes, 32 seconds compared with 8 minutes 49 seconds spent using the hand-list. Compared to the figures obtained from Apple, these data show a far higher level of engagement with the app when it was used in conjunction with the Cambridge Wall. Visitors were asked to rate how easy the resource was to use on a scale from 1 to 10, with 1 being classified as 'very easy' and 10 as 'very hard'. On average, visitors gave the app a score of 2 (easy) and the hardcopy a score of 4 (nearer the 'neither easy nor hard' banding). This could perhaps explain why visitors spent on average 3 minutes longer using the hand-list as the information was more difficult to access than through the app.

The App

What do you like about this resource?

The most common response, by one-third of respondents (13 of the 39 people interviewed), was that the app gave more information or greater detail than was otherwise available in the gallery. For example, one respondent commented, it 'provided lots of information, great background and knowledge of history of Cambridge'. Another stated, 'it allows me to get details of the things I am looking at'. One further person added that they liked 'getting information in front of you' and another thought that the app 'could be useful for non-experts'.

In addition to providing more information, further comments also focused on accessibility and choice. For example, five comments stated that the app allowed the visitor to select for themselves the objects they wanted to find out more about. A further three respondents commented on the way the app helped them to understand the layers of the display better. Five comments were from individuals who liked the accessibility of information, including one visitor who said it helped them 'access quickly what you are interested in' and another who said it was 'easier than reading a label, more practical'. Three people mentioned the extra audio features of the app including, 'like [the] audio, don't have to listen to everything – can pick bits', and another who said they liked the 'audio explanation of what [the] object is'. Finally, one visitor enjoyed the 'visual representation', and another preferred it to 'numbered labels'.

A smaller group of respondents focused on the relationship between the app and the display. One person liked the fact that you 'don't have to get too close to [the] case'. Two visitors commented on the display itself; one suggested they liked 'the form that objects are presented in' and the other enjoyed the 'display of shields'. Finally, five people commented on the 'interactivity' of the app, or that they liked the 'technology' more generally. Also, one visitor said that the app was 'modern and up-to-date'. Another response did not mention interactivity, but the visitor liked being 'able to engage with the display'.

How did it help you engage with the artefacts in the display?

Again, many comments to this question focused on the extra information provided by the app. Twelve people said they appreciated finding out more about the objects; 11 participants in the survey also mentioned that the app helped attract and hold people's attention and select objects to look at.

What problems did you have using the resource?

Fifteen people (38%) had no problems using the app. Three further individuals had few problems once it was explained how to use it. Five respondents found the iPad and case too heavy, with one commenting that it was 'awkward to hold due to weight'. Six people had problems choosing objects and small icons. One further visitor had difficulties with the touchscreen. Another found 'using the iPad and my camera [presumably at the same time] was challenging'.

If we could make three improvements to the resource, what would they be?

Eight people did not answer this question or said that no improvements were necessary. One individual commented that although the app was 'already good, a person leading me going through the objects will be great, but an iPad is good as well'.

Eight people requested more information to be available in the app, and two participants felt the app 'could be more interactive'. There were also several comments relating to the functionality of the app suggesting it 'could have come with more instructions'. Six people asked for headphones for the sound and seven comments were about better quality pictures or providing video. Finally, six comments asked for the app to be in languages other than English, with French, German and Italian requested. One person was also concerned 'about [the] security of [the] iPad, would someone take it?'

The Hand-list

What do you like about this resource?

Like the app, the most common response was that the hand-list gave extra information about objects in the case; this was mentioned by 36% of those interviewed (13 of the 36). For example, 'it provides [the] user with an understanding of stratigraphy and gives an idea of how material culture is stratified around/in Cambridge'. Three further comments about the additional information available in the hand-list were: 'helps put things in context', 'it is like a catalogue book, can look into different objects through the catalogue', 'can just pick out one or two things and find it in the catalogue'.

Six comments were related to the relationship between the case and the hand-list, such as, 'I like the spatial layout – depth in display between space and time. Also, like display map'. Seven comments focused on how easy or helpful the hand-list was: 'easy to read and find information'. Five people liked the 'pictures', 'illustrations', 'graphics' or 'colours' in the hand-list, with one visitor commenting that it 'makes you actually study it more closely, actually pay more attention, not just a cursory glance'. Three people provided negative comments in response to this question, saying that the hardcopy was: 'Hopeless. Very difficult to use', 'it's from the middle ages' or that they did not like it as it was 'difficult to follow'.

How did it help you engage with the artefacts in the display?

As with the previous question, the largest number of responses (10) concerned the extra information the resource provided. For example: 'gives background; more idea about where things come from'. Six people responded with comments about attention and engagement, such as: 'can search for different objects and realised the display is in layers of time' and 'made me more curious about what they were – pick a few that caught my eye, read more closely'. Three comments were about the details in the hardcopy; for instance one respondent commented: 'very good; precise; gives information'. Finally, a further three people thought the hand-list improved accessibility.

What problems did you have using the resource?

Only two visitors found no problems using the hand-list. People thought it was hard to match the objects on paper to the ones in the case. Visitors also struggled to identify both the age and geographic location of the objects, which perhaps can be summarised by two comments: 'it is not quite attractive reading', and it was 'hard to find information'. Several visitors requested a general introduction with instructions on how to use the hand-list and three people wanted more information. Finally, one visitor felt it was 'just a lot of detail – would need more time to read it properly, could be better for "the passing visitor"'.

If we could make three improvements to the resource, what would they be?

Four people did not answer this question or said they were 'not sure' what improvements could be made to the hand-list. Ten people asked for more or better information, for example: 'more information about what objects were used for, possible if fewer objects on a page'. Ten further comments sought guidance and explanation on how to use the resource. Improvements to the format of the book were requested by nine people. The most common comment though was to change the orientation of the list so that it 'opens like a regular book, not like a calendar'. Two people wanted it to be 'sturdier' or on 'thicker paper', with another two respondents adding that it 'looks worn'. One person also commented that it 'looks cheap'. One respondent asked for 'bigger fonts', and three comments requested 'languages other than English'. More information about numbering was asked for in four responses, with another visitor adding that they would like 'the description ... be on the glass ... like the ones upstairs'. Four people asked for the resource to be 'more accessible', one person added, 'maybe add a box of leaflets/hand-list next to the display'. One further comment asked for 'more than one copy' to be available. Four people asked for the resource to have bigger images or graphics. Finally, three people suggested the information should be made available in an interactive guide and two comments asked for 'more precise' or 'more refined' time periods.

Analysis of comments

More information

A previous visitor evaluation of the Cambridge Gallery conducted in 2013 asked 15 visitors how we could help them engage more with the objects (Harknett 2013). Of the ten people who responded to this question all asked for more information, dates and more detailed descriptions. Three visitors specifically requested this in relation to the Cambridge Wall display. Analysis of all evaluation data in 2013 revealed that 66% of all visitors to the museum requested more information, including appeals for basic data and resources such as dates, maps and timelines, but also information on how the artefacts were made and used. There were also requests for more information about context, as well as comparisons and connections between objects. But seemingly in direct contrast to these responses, tracking of visitors across the Cambridge Gallery revealed that text panels are not stopped at frequently. It is unlikely, therefore, that visitors will find the extra information they require through this traditional method. When all galleries from across the University of Cambridge Museums are compared the Cambridge Gallery has the lowest level of engagement with the text. Only 47% of visitors stopped at one or more of the text panels, compared with 56% in the Sedgwick Museum of Earth Sciences, 66% in the Origins of the Afro Comb exhibition at the Fitzwilliam Museum and 99% in the Polar Museum.

Thirty-three per cent of app users and 36% of hardcopy users felt the resource gave more information or greater detail. Additionally, 31% of app users and 28% of hand-list users liked the extra information the resource provided. In contrast with text panels, both the app and the hand-list seem to meet this need for more information better but, for many visitors, this was still not enough with 21% of app users and 28% of hardcopy users requesting more or better information.

Pick, Focus, Search

Eleven comments from app users were positive about the ability to 'pick', 'choose', or 'focus' on individual objects. Only two people used similar terms in the interviews about the hand-list. It seems that the physical act of selecting the artefact on the iPad affects users in a more profound way, encouraging engagement. Touching an object to get more information is a definite choice, compared to all the data being available at once on one sheet in the hand-list or on a text panel. Sometimes the hand-list even seemed to overwhelm people with data. Five hand-list users, but only one app user, used the term 'search' in relation to the resource. Only one was used in a negative sense but the more frequent use of the word appears significant. Only one visitor, an app user, referred specifically to an object: 'thought a lot more about the objects, *e.g.* how eel catcher worked; notice extra details'. This could be an area for future research, by asking visitors whether they had found any specific details of interest to see which objects, or snippets, are remembered after using the resource.

Time Spent by Age Group

The average time spent using the app and the hand-list was far greater than when the app was downloaded from Apple, reflecting high levels of engagement in conjunction with the Cambridge Wall display. People aged 24 and under spent the least time looking at the app, with the next two age categories spending similar amounts of time. All age groups looked at the hand-list for longer, but those visitors aged 50 and over spent the longest time.

Ease of Use Compared to Age of User

Those visitors aged 50 and over struggled most with the hand-list and found the app the easiest to use. Those aged 24 and under were the group who found the app the hardest to use. Thirteen visitors used the words 'quick' or 'easy' for the app; 9 visitors said the hand-list was 'easy' to use, but there were more negative comments about the hand-list than the app. Several people requested help to understand how the hand-list related to the display. Visitors were confused; they struggled to find artefacts and felt it took too long. For some users, the slower method of engaging with the resource was frustrating. They found it 'very difficult to use', 'difficult to follow', 'had to constantly check between display and catalogue'. One respondent even stated: 'a lot of time wasted trying to identify artefacts'. But for other visitors, the resource 'forced [them] to slow down and find it in the book'. On average, visitors spent 3 minutes 17 seconds less time using the app compared to the hand-list. As already mentioned, this could be a reflection of ease of use rather than implying that people were not as engaged with the app. When tracking took place in the gallery in 2013, visitors spent an average of 38 seconds at the Cambridge Wall (Harknett 2013). The participants in that tracking study did not know they were being evaluated. Time spent using both the app and hand-list was significantly greater, suggesting higher levels of engagement, but the participants to the survey also knew they were being observed. This may have, therefore skewed these timings. One might ask, for example, how long a visitor struggling to use the hand-list might have persevered on their own before their patience ran out.

Future Use of Resources

Based on this evaluation we are taking steps to improve the ease of usage of the app and hand-list, including training new volunteer staff how to use them and providing an extra iPad loaded with the app for use by the public facilitated by gallery staff. Also, a sheet explaining how to use the hand-list has been added to the front of the resource. A desirable feature which could be added in the future would be to provide a link to our online museum catalogue so that visitors could access information about similar artefacts in the collections that are not on display. This is especially important for an institution where such a small proportion of the collections are on public display.

'Look, Look Again': Making Museum Visitors Work

Museums are increasingly working towards generating more engaging visitor experiences with digital technologies such as social media at the forefront of these initiatives (Decker 2015a; 2015b). Many museums have developed apps for use in their galleries, especially embracing mobile technology to achieve this. Quoting the Museums and Mobile Survey 2012, according to Fisher and Moses, '… 75% of museums surveyed planning to develop mobile experiences have as a primary goal "to provide additional interpretative information for visitors"' (Fisher & Moses 2013, 3). 'Engaging with visitors' and providing 'a more interactive experience' were also seen as important motivations (Fisher & Moses 2013, 3). We certainly had the same goals when developing the app and hand-list and evaluation has shown us that both resources have been successful in providing visitors with more information. But what about 'engaging with visitors' and 'providing a more interactive experience'? As Fisher and Moses go on to explain, the jury is still out in terms of whether apps and other types of digital resource distract visitors from interacting with exhibits (Fisher & Moses 2013, 3). If, as a previous MAA survey has shown (Harknett 2013), visitors already do not read the information available to them in galleries on display panels, will they read the extra information provided on museum apps (Fisher & Moses 2013, 3)? A key question when assessing the utility of digital technology in museums is does it work better than traditional analogue methods of audience engagement? In the context of this paper, does the app engage audiences better than the hand-list? Through our evaluation, we have found that both resources increased engagement by making visitors work, as they were encouraged to look between the resource and the display and look again. The difference between the app and the hand-list was that the app did this more effectively as the work required of the visitor did not generally develop into frustration as it sometimes did with the hand-list.

Lessons Learned

The Museum of Archaeology and Anthropology, Cambridge, is a small institution with an even smaller budget for digital projects but despite this, one of the biggest lessons learned is the need for adequate account in any project for evaluation and greater provision for marketing. Data obtained from so-called digital analytics allowed the Museum to assess in a limited way how the app was used outside of the museum. Still, it is no replacement for visitor evaluation. Low numbers of downloads for the app caused initial concern, and in retrospect, it should have been promoted more widely, but numbers of users are not always the best measure of success. For example, a project using the online photo-sharing service Instagram and aimed at increasing public engagement and interest in a new display of the Fossil Hall at the American National Museum of Natural History, an institution attracting 20,000 visitors a day, received only 70 photographs. Significantly, it also generated passionate and enduring interest amongst a small group of visitors (Chen *et al.* 2015). It is clear from our audience evaluations that a number of users took a lot away from their use of both the app and the hand-list and engaged closely with the display through these resources. Given that, the app cost in excess of £10,000 to develop and requires an expensive iPad. Digital products also have notoriously short lifespans (Decker 2015c, 6). The hand-list, which was cheap to produce, was extremely good value for money and underlines the continuing value of analogue resources, especially to small institutions.

Conclusion

In conclusion, it is argued that museum resources and particularly apps can encourage visitor engagement if they require visitors to work: to look, pick, focus and search. As Hennessey and Corso expressed it, what makes these types of resources and initiatives successful '... is not the information that the technology provides or the multidisciplinary approach conveying it, but rather that the technology serves as a tool, one that visitors already use in their everyday lives, to engage in a conversation' (Hennessey & Corso 2015, 20). Mobile technologies are surely the future, as they will allow visitors to explore information about museum collections using their own devices: to curate one's own experience (Decker 2015c, 5). But as we have seen with the hand-list, analogue resources can be successful. It is also important to consider the visitor experience and how they relate to museum exhibits when developing digital technology. There is little point in bombarding visitors with more and more information unless they access and process it. One way to achieve this is to create digital resources that encourage visitors to look at exhibits, to seek and focus on the information that interests them.

Postscript

In the autumn of 2019, we received notification from Apple that as it had not been updated for some time, the Cambridge Wall app no longer conformed to App Store guidelines. We later had notification from the University of Cambridge that, as a result of this and because of its low download figures, they had decided to withdraw its online support for the app. Unfortunately, we were unable to find funds to update the app and, from late 2019, it has no longer been available for download. We hope at some point in the future to update and reinstate the app for free download. In the meantime, the app remains in use in the museum's galleries, but without an update, it is unclear how long it will work effectively even in the museum environment. Its use is probably restricted to the lifespan of the iPads currently in use.

Given that the average life of a museum exhibit at MAA is around 30 years it is clear that, with the rapid development and evolution of digital technology, the two have different life trajectories. Levelling the lifespans of physical displays and digital technology in museums remains a significant challenge. Even with more rapid renewal of displays, digital technology would ideally need to work effectively for at least 10–15 years.

Download and usage statistics for the app from January 2015 to September 2019 can be summarised as follows:

- 2122 product page views
- 668 downloads
- 1.47 monthly average sessions per active device

App units by territory:
- 248 USA
- 120 UK
- 101 Australia
- 32 Canada
- 20 China Mainland

References

Chen, C., Lindsay J. L., Starrs S. & Stauffer B. W. (2015) Closing the Fossil Hall and opening Fotorama! Online and onsite engagement at the National Museum of Natural History. In J. Decker (ed.), *Engagement and Access: Innovative Approaches for Museums,* 81–9. London, Rowman & Littlefield.

Decker, J. (ed.) (2015a) *Engagement and Access: Innovative Approaches for Museums.* London, Rowman & Littlefield.

Decker, J. (ed.) (2015b) *Technology and Digital Initiatives: Innovative Approaches for Museums.* London, Rowman & Littlefield.

Decker, J. (2015c) Introduction. In J. Decker (ed.), *Technology and Digital Initiatives: Innovative Approaches for Museums,* 1–11. London, Rowman & Littlefield.

Elliott, M. & Thomas, N. (2011) *Gifts and Discoveries: The Museum of Archaeology and Anthropology, Cambridge.* London, Scala.

Fisher, M. & Moses, J. (2013) *Rousing the Mobile Herd: Apps that Encourage Real Space Engagement. Museums and the Web 2013,* 1–20. www.mw2013.museumandtheweb.com/paper/rousing-the-mobile-herd-apps-that-encourage-real-space-engagement/ (accessed 15 June 2016).

Hennessey, W. & Corso, A. (2015) Listening to our audiences. In J. Decker (ed.), *Engagement and Access: Innovative Approaches for Museums,* 17–25. London, Rowman & Littlefield.

Harknett, S.-J. (2013) *Museum of Archaeology and Anthropology: Cambridge Gallery.* Cambridge, unpublished report, Museum of Archaeology and Anthropology.

Harknett, S.-J. (2016) *Analogue and Digital Comparison, Museum of Archaeology and Anthropology.* Cambridge, unpublished report, Museum of Archaeology and Anthropology

Smith, P. J. (2009) *A "Splendid Idiosyncrasy": Prehistory at Cambridge 1915-50.* Oxford, British Archaeological Report 485.

Chapter 5

Music as a Means of Opening up Archaeological Museums to New Audiences: The Morning Concerts at the National Archaeological Museum, Athens (2014)

Ariadne Klonizaki

Under the title of *Morning Concerts at the Museum* in May 2014, the National Archaeological Museum of Athens started an experiment: a cycle of concerts held in the Museum's Altar Hall, which is the largest of the Museum's sculpture collection galleries. The exhibits in this room are configured to convey the impression of an ancient open-air sanctuary with the central space occupied by a large early 2nd-century BC marble altar from Athens standing on a base, surrounded by votive statuettes and reliefs from a variety of sanctuaries. These include works by eminent sculptors as well as simpler dedications to various gods and heroes, especially to Hercules, Aphrodite, the Nymphs and Pan. The Altar Hall has traditionally been used as a venue for events.

On Wednesday 3 December 2014, during the second cycle of the music project which opened with the song-cycle *Winterreise* by Franz Schubert, the newspaper *Kathimerini* emphasised the:

> will of the National Archaeological Museum, the first and biggest Museum of the country … to offer something more to those who find their way to its premises and, why not, keep them a bit longer into the exhibition halls. And the public did respond; senior visitors who take their morning stroll around the area of the museum, tourists, mothers with young children, attended enthusiastically for an hour to listen to good music … This has been one of the most pleasant initiatives taken by a public museum, especially in the mornings, insofar as it does not disturb the visitors, on the contrary, it enthuses them. Everything is done with respect, and it is for this very reason that is so well received. It is a way for NAM to attract new audiences and bring them closer.

This description by journalist Yiota Sykka corresponds to a large extent to the actual composition of the audience that attended these events. It also accurately portrays the museum's effort to make a difference in a period of economic crisis by offering quality cultural activities aiming not only at an audience numbers increase but also at the expansion of the museum's public engagement opportunities.

The series of *Morning Concerts at the Museum* were initiated in May 2014 by the Museum's Department of Public Relations and Educational Programmes (Fig. 5.1). The concerts followed a specific code of conduct:

- Organised by the staff of the National Archaeological Museum, during May and December.
- Conducted within the regular opening hours of the Museum, every Wednesday at noon in the Altar Hall.
- They included the participation of renowned professional musicians in the events.
- Careful choice of small classical music ensembles and classical Greek composers.
- The artists agree to perform voluntarily and the artistic content of the concerts was a collaboration between them and the Museum.
- None of the Museum's operations were compromised during the concert, a condition about which the artists were informed beforehand.
- Concerts were performed without microphonic systems or other kinds of amplifiers.
- Musical ensembles could rehearse, often on the eve of the concert itself, during the opening hours of the Museum.
- Every concert could sit 40–70 participants, on a flexible layout in the Altar Hall, requiring minimum set-up time.

Figure 5.1: Franz Schubert, Die Winterreise, D 911. *Baritone: Kostas Raphailidis, piano: Frixos Mortzos (photo: A. Klonizaki, December 2014).*

- A bilingual (Greek/English) programme was issued for each event, kindly sponsored by the Society of the Friends of the National Archaeological Museum.
- The entire project was run with minimum cost for the Museum.
- Free attendance to concerts for Museum visitors was included in the museum's admission.
- Events were promoted through the Museum's website, through press releases and on public radio.

The first series included five concerts in May 2014, followed by the second series, with four more concerts, in December 2014. The highlight of the series was the final concert on Christmas day in December 2014, during which the Altar Hall reached its highest possible capacity, attracting approximately 200 visitors. The Museum intends that this type of music events will be repeated regularly, in the same place and at the same time of the year during regular opening hours. So far, the nine concerts have hosted 35 professional artists of very high standards, who in their majority collaborate with the Greek National Opera. The concert programmes included both Greek and Western European chamber music. Although the Museum led the development of this project, one of the Museum's intentions was to co-curate these events with the artists, who were invited to select the content of the artistic programme. This emphasis on creative freedom and co-curation enhanced the musical integrity and appeal of the concerts, but also enabled the Museum to develop an alternative cultural offer by exploring new partnerships for its audiences at a time of severe economic pressure.

The audience of the concerts included a) Museum visitors who were surprised by the event taking place on the day of their visit and b) members of the public who came that day to the Museum aiming specifically to attend the concert. The musicians were in close contact with the public during the concerts. Working with performers in a public museum space during opening hours might have curatorial challenges, which are likely to require quick problem-solving and improvisation skills by museum staff; the experience, however, opens up opportunities for new encounters in the museum context. Many of the participating artists, usually accustomed to performing in concert halls, found the experience and relationship they developed with the Museum during the music events, very special: '... I went away with the best of impressions already from the eve of the concert, that is the day of the rehearsal, which was also conducted during visiting hours; a fact that created an even stronger sense of spontaneity as it took pleasantly by surprise the visitors and quite a few of them recognized and whispered among themselves (quite close to me) the names of the composers whose works we were playing, those of Erik Satie and Claude Debussy' says pianist Maria Aloupi.

However, planning and delivery of the concerts was not without challenges. One of these was that not all museum visitors favoured the concert while on a regular museum visit where they anticipated the well-known to them 'museum silence'

Figure 5.2: Concert of the ATTIKA Plucked String Orchestra (Ορχήστρα Νυκτών Εγχόρδων), Tenor: Yiannis Christopoulos (photo: A. Klonizaki, May 2014) https://www.youtube.com/watch?v=4_cf-DW32X4&list=RD4_cf-DW32X4&index=1.

(Fig. 5.2). 'Such a concert presents a considerable challenge since the artist has to attract an unsuspecting audience, which has not come on purpose to attend the performance and, therefore, may not be interested at all. I was very happy, however, to notice the gradual, but continuously increasing attendance at the venue. Visitors gradually gather around the area where the musicians interpret their music, forming something like a theatre circle, some seated, others standing, a micro-environment of different atmospheres inside the Museum' said Sofia Kontossi, one of the pianists participating at the concert series.

Because of the selected music genre and style, and building of the concert programme, in harmony with the museum collections, the relatively short duration of the event and intervention into the flow of visitors to the Altar Hall, the museum did not receive any negative visitor observations or comments throughout the series. With the assistance of the experienced Museum security personnel visitors were moving around unobstructed while none of the exhibits became inaccessible to them during the event. We could say that the concert was seen by the visitors as an opportunity for relaxation and entertainment; a moment that built an emotional connection with the museum and its exhibits.

The following conclusions – and challenges – arose from our experience:

- Archaeological museums are associated with specific ideas and their collections are associated with national value. Projects that introduce interventions to national museums bear symbolic meaning. They constitute multiple meaning-making encounters that do not stem from the archaeological collection solely.
- The way to implement public engagement programmes, such as the above, during periods of economic difficulty, is to establish strong partnerships. Embedded into this perspective was the eagerness to contribute and the expertise of the Museum staff. Equally was the willingness of the artists to facilitate co-curation and promote the success of the musical mornings. Despite the financial restraints of the country during that time such partnerships have opened up opportunities for exploration and creative thinking within heritage contexts and formed connections between archaeological context and musical content. Many of the artists have the desire to present programmes inspired by the Greek antiquity, and the Altar Hall exhibits, in particular. One of the Museum's ultimate goals, therefore, was to incorporate music performances into the interpretation of museum objects.
- Music became a new reason to access the Museum space. A rise to about 80% in the number of visitors accessing the Museum, between December 2013 and December 2014 was a result – among other factors – of the Wednesday music project and its promotion in printed and electronic press, blogs and social media. Successful implementation of such activities generates a new loyal audience to the archaeological museum.
- By organising high-quality cultural events, the Museum also elevates itself to a cultural institution in the city in a field other than that of archaeological heritage. Other music events that have taken place at the Museum forecourt effectively contribute, we believe, to the upgrading of this – recently challenged – area in the centre of Athens. With their popular character, they aim for a wider audience and transform the forecourt into a public square, a point of reference in the city centre.
- There is substantial potential to expand collaboration schemes established through the morning concerts, to increase the number of visitors, as well as attract commercial partners (*e.g.* the Athens Hotel Association, Unions of Tourist Agents etc).
- The National Archaeological Museum has cultivated an appetite for quality events that can now act as a beacon for the establishment of other events and public engagement actions, addressed to different public groups currently under-represented in the Museum's audiences. Reaching out to more diverse audience types comes as a more significant challenge, bringing together people who would not usually visit archaeological museums or attend classical music concerts. To a certain extent the NAM has already achieved that; concerts were enjoyed by different

age and class groups and were particularly well received by families with young children.

- Offering high-quality music events is a social contribution to the public since this 2-in-1 opportunity (visit to the Museum and music event attendance) at a reasonable price improves the quality of city life. The fact that schools got interested in attending the concerts demonstrates that this activity fulfils a social need on the part of school audiences. We, therefore, can also offer meaning-making opportunities within events, which are not mere educational activities.

- The music programme contributes to and strengthens the scope and role of a national museum that belongs to its citizens, particularly during the times of economic crisis. It further provides evidence that such projects can be sustainable and can have a high impact on museum audiences. The Museum is keen to continue and augment the project, secure its frequency and maintain its high-quality standards. The experience could also be transferable to other landmark Greek museums and could further create the conditions for collaboration with other European archaeological museums and museums housing Ancient World collections.

The connection of the past to the present brings together a loyal audience that gets closer to the antiquities, makes the Museum a familiar space, and develops a vital association with it. 'The past has no meaning if deprived of any connection to the present. In the morning concerts exactly, this miracle happened' said a visitor, Nena Mouratoglou. National archaeological museums are still perceived as traditional and static entities. It is as much about the lack of meaning-making possibilities and exhibition modalities, as it is about what we believe these museums represent. Transforming the nature of the National Archaeological Museum to a more interactive and inclusive one was made possible through music. Widening the focus of heritage interpretation and taking on a fresh approach led to partnerships of co-curation. Seeing ourselves as enablers and not as the museum experts in an innovative model, we managed to: a) attract more visitors and new audiences, b) develop engagement opportunities, c) turned economic restriction into an opportunity and possibility for new, meaningful collaborations. Fostering meaning-making experiences is and should be at the heart of every museum's mission and activities. Employing an artistic interpretive approach has laid the foundation for a constructive shift in the relationship between our museum and its audience. Our experience with The Morning Concerts at the National Archaeological Museum of Athens has shown that planning and implementing for an active audience can be beneficial for all parties involved.

Acknowledgements

The concerts initiative was fully supported by the Director of the NAM, Dr Maria Lagogianni-Georgakarakos (December 2014), and the Acting Director of the NAM, Dr George Kakavas (May 2014). I would like to extend my warmest thanks to Dr Areti Galani,

Pandelis Feleris, Labrini Tsitsou, Dr Sofia Kontossi, Konstantina Polychronopoulou, Dr Evangelos Vivliodetis, Dr Despina Ignatiadou, Dr Kostas Paschalidis, Bessy Drougka, Kelly Drakomathioulaki, my colleagues at the NAM and all the performers.

Further Reading

Hooper-Greenhill, E. (1992) *Museums and the Shaping of Knowledge.* London & New York, Routledge.

Rodney, H. (2013) *Heritage: Critical Approaches.* London, Routledge.

Satwicz, T. & Morrissey, K. (2011) Public curation: from trend to research-based practice. In B. Adair, B. Filene & L. Koloski (eds), *Letting Go? Sharing Historical Authority in a User-Generated World*, 196–204. Walnut Creek, CA, Pew Center for Arts & Heritage.

Silverman, L. (2010) Visitor meaning-making in museums for a new age. *Curator: The Museum Journal* 38, 161–70.

Weil, S. (2007) The museum and the public. In S. Watson (ed.), *Museums and their Communities*, 32–46. London, Routledge.

Chapter 6

Experiments in Interpretation

N. James

Helping to oversee the university's Fitzwilliam Museum in the mid-1800s, William Whewell, a leading professor at Cambridge, came to regard its displays as experiments in presentation (Burn 2016, 80). Converging with him in the wake of 'the new museology', Albano has extended the principle to visitors' reception of art: 'The experimental exhibition implies a reflection on what is contemporary art and', indeed, she adds, 'contemporary science'. What 'legitimacy and authority' have either museums or laboratories, then, 'as sites of knowledge production in which ... actors concur in generating meaning' (Albano 2018, 113)? Nor does everyone necessarily agree: if the function of galleries has changed 'from ... representation to ... encounter', remark Basu and Macdonald (2007, 14, 16), then visitors sifting 'realms of proliferating knowledges and surfeits of information' can now assess for themselves the merits of 'competing truths'.

The principle is expressed nicely by the term 'experimentarium' for one of the Estonian History Museum's galleries (no doubt borrowed from the popular science centre in Denmark; James 2013, 271). Whewell would have been intrigued by how often, today, a larger or better-funded museum can mount temporary exhibitions. For they are opportunities both to promote the museum and to test technical options for permanent displays. 'Experiment' and 'experience' derive from the Latin for 'to try out'. So does 'expert'; and Swain (2007, 297) points out that active visitors will interpret archaeological exhibits variously. The don who ordained the term 'scientist' would hardly have taken that seriously, but we do now.

Options for offering us an 'encounter' were demonstrated in a sample of five temporary exhibitions of archaeology, shown in Europe between 2010 and 2016. Before describing them, it may be helpful to sum up what curators now think they know about conditions affecting visitors' responses in a gallery (Black 2005, 129–50, 179–210, 271–86).

Variables

A display's success depends on three conditions. Visitors' capacities and priorities are the most basic, including age and cultural grounding. Then the exhibits and the theme of presentation must match our interests adequately; and, thirdly, the design must be compatible and stimulating.

In effect, an exhibition should declare 'Here is something interesting or important for you'. Since the past is more-or-less unlike the present, archaeological exhibits seem curious, either because they look strange or because, for all their antiquity, they seem familiar. An appropriate balance is needed between familiarity and surprise. The exhibition should intrigue us, but it should not baffle us.

The second factor is the exhibition's question or message. It can be stated explicitly, or it can be left implicit. Interpretation of the exhibits may be didactic, or it may be open-ended. We could be invited to engage directly with the exhibits; or to consider the methods on which discovery and analysis of archaeological finds depend; or even, in theory, to assess the exhibition as an exhibition (Albano 2018, 99; King & Marstine 2006).

Thirdly, the exhibition's mood should match visitors'. It should suit the footing on which we enter the gallery, or it must persuade us to adjust to its own tone. It helps if the gallery itself suggests 'Here is something interesting'. Space must be conducive: its size and form, architectural style, the acoustic, perhaps the temperature. That is usually the designer's purpose in decorating or adapting the gallery for an exhibition.

Then the exhibition must hold our attention, intriguing us with a set of principles for thinking about the exhibits. There should be an issue with a method for assessing it; like a puzzle or a game. The presentation can help to absorb us: variety of exhibits – larger and smaller, for example, different colours; variation in spacing, mounting and lighting; complementary or supplementary illustrations such as replicas; various media of interpretation, audial as well as text, for example, to engage different faculties or aptitudes. To keep us engaged, the tone may vary. It often does in larger exhibitions. Yet the task is to stimulate us without letting the design or medium distract from the exhibits and the exhibition's topic or message.

However we engage with it, the exhibition should encourage a coherent 'flow' of attention (Hooper-Greenhill 1994, 153–9). Howard Gardner has helped to account for (if not explain) what engages (or fails to engage) one visitor or another by distinguishing eight 'intelligences' variously distributed amongst us (Davis *et al.* 2011): sensitivity to rhythm; verbal, linguistic or literary skills; counting and logic; visual sensitivity; alertness to the physical environment; kinetic capacities; alertness to others; and awareness of self. Thus, an exhibition deploying diverse stimuli could satisfy different visitors in various ways and all the more a group sharing the experience.

Of the exhibitions to be considered here, one was the display and interpretation of a medieval chest and its contents; and another showed finds associated with medieval and Early Modern pubs. One used a striking variety of media to evoke a Roman town in Turkey. A fourth showed prehistoric figurines from Europe and Japan. The other exhibition was about ancient and Early Modern warfare in Europe and the Middle East. It was dominated by a display of skeletons that some criticised, at the time, as a blatant affront to decency.

Thought

Was it better to have offended than to leave us indifferent? Exhibitions of archaeology should prompt thought even if the past that they reveal was nasty. They should encourage 'critical thinking', exposing our assumptions about the world, what it has been and, by extension, perhaps, what it could become.

The 'challenge', confirmed interpreters' evangelist, Freeman Tilden (1977, 91), is 'to put your visitor in possession of at least one disturbing idea'. We should be glad, then, to let the disquiet linger beyond the gallery (Basu & Macdonald 2007, 17, 13). Didactic exhibitions are widely out of favour now but visitors have complained about certain presentations of late, that they are too open-ended. Arguably, exhibitions should offer at least a couple of interpretive options (James 2013, 271–2); but considerable ingenuity is demanded for openness to succeed on visitors' terms as well as – let alone rather than – the archaeologists' (Shanks & Tilley 1992, 97–8).

Each of the exhibitions to be considered here depended on sowing doubt by creating, if not also resolving, a tension. The exhibitions on figurines and the Roman town assigned complementary interpretive functions to distinct parts of the gallery. The one about inns simply withheld explicit explanation. Especially there, the resulting tension helped to expose how we were construing the exhibits, perhaps encouraging us to respond more consciously to less familiar items. The presentation of the figurines, likewise, went so far as to raise an issue as to what the past was – or is.

That was disconcerting, of course, for the archaeologist (James & Chippindale 2010); but Carman (2002, 17–9) helps to explain the issue. He distinguishes finds as 'resources', surviving for archaeologists to study today, from the 'record' of what happened in the past as inferred by their studies. Then he distinguishes professional interests in the record and the resource from lay evaluations which may spring from all sorts of concerns, not necessarily pertaining to the past; and, for this third value, he uses the term 'heritage'. The figurines were presented as heritage in this sense.

Science?

The very purpose of that exhibition was to expose the relativity of knowledge. Held in the Sainsbury Centre for Visual Arts, at the University of East Anglia, England, in 2010, *Unearthed* compared prehistoric figurines from south-eastern Europe and Japan (James & Chippindale 2010). Faced with issues in both epistemology and ethics, social science has retreated from comparison over the past 40 years but, in large part, the curators avoided them by inviting visitors to interpret the figurines – gratifyingly strange to behold – without necessarily considering where they were from or even how old they were.

The Centre's striking architecture was used to distinguish evidence from interpretation. On one side of the building were displayed the figurines while the other was used to show miniatures from different parts of the world and various kinds of modern doll alongside ancient Japanese specimens from the university's own collection. The first side was provided with certain discreet prompts, such as 'women may have had power and agency'; but, as though to insist on the integrity of the exhibits there, in and of themselves, and to query archaeological expertise, it was on the second side that some account was given of the scientific research that yields ancient finds; and here too, on the second side, were quoted comments on ancient figurines by various archaeologists along with remarks on miniatures and toys by the likes of Man Ray, Walter Benjamin, Guy Debord, Antony Gormley and Will Self, a photograph of Frida Kahlo holding an ancient Mexican figurine, and some of Jonah Samson's voyeurist compositions. Added around the gallery were figures placed by Andrew Cochrane as anomalies, to further disturb any preconceptions about expertise or professional interpretive authority (Cochrane & Russell 2007). Here, indeed, were 'knowledges and ... information' galore (Basu & Macdonald 2007, 16).

Archaeological research notwithstanding, averred *Unearthed*, the figurines 'remain mysterious'. On that basis, it tried to prompt 'personal responses'. So also shown (in the first part of the exhibition) were clay models made by visitors in response to a previous exhibition of ancient Japanese figurines. The catalogue affirmed that artistic and literary rumination 'can elicit significances just as valid as' archaeologists' deductions (Unearthed Team 2010, 2); and Bailey *et al.* (2010, 155) nudged us, for good measure, by asking 'Is this good enough? Is this science?'.

Guidance

In contrast, the exhibition of the chest sought to inculcate a professional value for 'heritage' and to recommend particular interpretations. Recently recovered from the waters off Tallinn harbour, it was shown in a single modest gallery in 2011–2 (James 2013, 271–2). The surviving contents – weights and a set of scales, coins, a bell, knife handles of wood and bone, fragmentary leather sheaths – were mounted beside the chest. Also displayed, to provide context, were medieval sheaths, soles, a mitten and pots. Held at the central branch of the Estonian History Museum, this was the most conventional of the five exhibitions. *Watertight Sources* offered little openness.

It posed two sets of questions. Among the first was 'What should I do if I find a historical item?'. For there is anxiety in Estonia, now, about unauthorised disturbance of archaeological remains. The second issue was the interpretation of the chest. It was posed by reference to the coins: 135 from Visby, over the Baltic Sea, dating from the 1220s to the 1280s, but also 62 pennies of 1265–1332 from Tallinn. Alternatives were offered: considering Tallinn's commercial history, the numismatist ascribed the chest to a local Hanseatic merchant; but the curator envisaged a foreigner hopping among Baltic ports. The soles, mitten and pots suggested a palpable domestic story, but the exhibition guided us, instead, to the economic history. It directed us but, by showing how experts can disagree, it sought to demonstrate that interpretation is always likely to be provisional.

Then, held at the same museum's Maarjamäe Palace branch, *Poriveski Kõrts* (politely translatable as *Muck Mill Tavern*) showed finds from waterlogged medieval and Early Modern cess pits (James 2013, 274–5). They were selected as the sort of things that would have been used in a tavern (*kõrts*). Shown in 2011–2, this was the smallest of the five exhibitions. It had two parts. The first displayed wooden balls, a skittle, knuckle bones (astragali) for gaming, bone flutes, bone and ceramic figurines, a purse and coins, all mounted on boards painted à la Brueghel the Elder with an impression of the edge of Tartu and its outskirts. A low door through a wooden partition led into the second part, rows of tables and the mock-up of a fireplace surrounded by walls with paintings of customers and staff. With a recording of 'early music' to suggest entertainment, the tables and the floor between them were strewn with candlesticks, more knuckle bones, dice, tuning pegs and a jew's harp, a firkin and spiles, crockery and cutlery, food bones and potsherds, a small brick and certain other inscrutable items, as though 'down the pub' in mid-evening. Replicas of food, more crockery, a barrel and playing cards fleshed out the archaeology. We entered a passage between the displays where there was a table like the ones supporting the exhibits. It had chairs and a board for us to play Nine Men's Morris.

Also on the table was the small catalogue. Otherwise, there was not a single word of text. The catalogue was the only source of explicit explanation. *Kõrts* opened interpretation widely to us, thus. The setting, of course, and the scatter of exhibits went a long way to explaining the scene as cheerful hospitality; but the enigmatic pieces helped to prevent us from depending simply on preconceptions about pubs.

Dream

The exhibition on the Roman town depended on staging too but with much more space and great force. *Sagalassos: City of Dreams* was shown at the Gallo-Roman Museum in Tongeren, Belgium, also in 2011–2 (James 2012). Occupied from the Hellenistic period to the Middle Ages, Sagalassos was 'Antioch in Pisidia', western Turkey (*Acts* Chapters 13–4). The centre was developed under the Emperors Hadrian and Marcus Aurelius and again in the early 400s. Yet the region is prone to earthquakes and, with particular attention to the complicated effects on the archaeology, the exhibition dwelt on the damage and disruption endured in about 500 and the early 600s. *Sagalassos* was larger than *Unearthed* and much bigger than the Estonian exhibitions.

Starting with the feet, lower right leg and head from a gigantic statue of Marcus Aurelius, assembled in anatomical position to show the figure's original height, most of the exhibits were mounted amongst scaffolding which divided them by age and theme and helped to direct us to one corner. There, signs drew us along a blank corridor to a dark vault with the fragmentary frieze of a dance and some indistinct shapes in the background. That led along a passage covered with printed calls of distress. Pulling aside a curtain at the end of it revealed a chamber, throbbing with the chorus in Stravinsky's *Oedipus Rex*, where, after adjusting our eyes to the dimness, we made out the shapes of twisted corpses on the floor. Then the other shapes glimpsed vaguely along the corridor resolved themselves into sculptures above a pool of flowing water and, spotlit, the white face of the fertility goddess suspended over a bed of red poppies. Through an ambiguous gloom, between tilting walls, we found the corner of a potter's workshop with sherds scattered across collapsed shelving. Here the buckled walls supported a ramp like the side of a fallen building. Clambering up it to peer at a bust of Zeus, and then teetering back down, was a novel experience, in a gallery. Finally, we entered a bright stark white chamber where scaffolding supported the gigantic marble foot, lower leg and head from a statue of Hadrian, laid out horizontally.

Sagalassos was designed with the help of opera director, Guy Joosten. Again like *Kõrts*, it left the core of the interpretive task to the visitor. It deftly minimised what one could have expected from an archaeology museum. The name, Antioch, was not mentioned in the principal texts, labels and videos. Nor did the exhibition exploit common Belgian knowledge of Tongeren's own prominence during the Roman era to explain Sagalassos's context in the Empire. Nor was there a catalogue.

To the contrary, *Sagalassos* left us to make sense of how the exhibits and the exposition of methodology amongst the stark scaffolding were juxtaposed with the melodramatic evocation of disaster in the second section. With labels in Belgium's three official languages plus English and, for the benefit of so many of its immigrants, Turkish, it felt as though the museum was quite prepared for us to follow the implications beyond the archaeology to contemporary economic and political affairs.

Shock

Turned from the horizontal to vertical, 45 human skeletons were tightly stretched out for us to see straight on, with two from bodies which had been flung across the rest. Neatly set out below were musket balls and artillery shot. Owing, perhaps, to such clinical arrangement, or the unfamiliar angle, or perhaps to the exhibit's sturdy frame, dispassionately marked 'Lützen, 6. November 1632', the horror seemed only to register later, after seeing many more bones and weapons both modern and ancient.

It was the opening display in *Krieg* (*War*), shown at the Prehistory Museum in Halle, Germany, in 2015–6 (James 2016). Sub-titled 'an archaeological search for traces', it went on to explain the Battle of Lützen and its context in the Thirty Years' War before showing evidence for warfare from prehistoric Europe and the Dynastic eras in Egypt and Mesopotamia and films of combat among chimpanzees and New Guinea highlanders. This was the largest of the five exhibitions.

Reception of *Krieg* seems to have been mixed. A minority of critics expressed dismay about the bones from Lützen. Pointing out that, as Christians, the victims must have 'hoped to find rest in consecrated ground' and that those killed in European wars have been buried with respect since the 1860s, Ivan Gaskell (2016) urged that 'responsibility to the dead requires their re-interment without exposure to the public gaze'. At one there with archaeologists in North America, Australia and Britain, he concluded that, especially confronting us so face on, the opening display was gratuitous 'sensationalism'.

The offending skeletons were among 125 excavated from a pit at the battlefield. The bodies had been stripped and all but the last two packed into rows and layers. It was, at least in part, that efficiency that was so disturbing; and it was surely to reflect that orderliness that the curators had lined up the ammunition beneath. The same quality was then implied, among other exhibits, by demonstrating apparently standardised types of prehistoric weaponry and showing the serried personnel on the Sumerian Standard of Ur. The theme was collective discipline. So, the point of the opening display was less the dead themselves than what it showed about the institutions that had brought them into battle and then disposed of their remains.

Citing Tilden's dictum (1977, 9) that 'The chief aim of Interpretation is not instruction, but provocation', Uzzell (1989, 46) has argued that museums should both celebrate our 'finest achievements' and 're-present the more shameful events of our past'; and that to be moved by seeing 'medals ... guns or ... mutilated bodies' 'can be a source of social good'; so that sometimes interpretation 'has to be shocking'. The general impression of visitors leaving 'Krieg' was not titillation but sombre thoughtfulness.

Engagement

The five exhibitions tried to catch and hold our attention in various ways. Four sought to suggest interpretation by making a distinctive setting of or in the gallery. Of course, we had to recognise the scenery. One wondered, in *Sagalassos*, whether the red poppies connoted the same to Belgians as to Turks; and the risk in *Kõrts* was that lack of explanation would make it too difficult to understand the set for any visitors from countries without a tradition of pubs. All five exhibitions did sow a thread of curiosity or doubt – or, in *Krieg*, perhaps incredulity – to draw us from start to end. Four of them went so far as to stir tension between scientific assessment and subjective response. Four engaged us with elements of play.

For *Krieg*, other than lighting, nothing was done to modify the gallery. The museum's neoclassical style seemed ironically indifferent to the displays. The exhibition itself was diverse: exhibits large and small, a chamber devoted to the death of the Swedish king at Lützen, reconstructions of whole prehistoric burials, life-size reproductions of rock art, some striking artists' impressions of battle, videos. The impact depended on that first sight of the skeletons and then the effect of so much kit for violence in what followed. The opening display's bland frame and the rows of carefully manufactured prehistoric weapons seemed to match the mechanical way in which the corpses had been interred at Lützen. In the same way, anthropologists' technical assessments of the bones were juxtaposed with the evidence of how the dead had been handled that day.

If *Krieg* was minimalist, the simplest example of how mounting in itself can suggest interpretation was *Kõrts*. Its set was the only obvious source of guidance. Partly because it eschewed labels, the presentation was very open-ended but, presumably, visitors' interpretations were expected to converge based on prior experience. Certain ambiguous exhibits may have helped to focus the attention and we could immerse ourselves more by settling down to the board game.

In contrast, *Watertight* showed an early map of Tallinn's harbour and a film of the divers but few other pictures. There was a soundtrack of the divers at work, with their aqualungs, indistinct but, like the music in *Kõrts*, conveying mood – here, attentive, presumably to reinforce the message about proper archaeological recovery. By the same token, although one of the closing texts urged that 'History leaves plenty of room for interpretation', the two expert assessments implied that the scope is limited.

With its scene of disaster, *Sagalassos*, of course, was the most obviously theatrical. Guy Joosten explained in one of the videos that the problem had been to evoke a whole town inside the gallery; but his solution to that challenge achieved a lot more. The potter's shop looked much messier than the set for *Kõrts*. Few gallery-goers will have seen flowing water in an exhibition. We were made to pick our way through a stage set furnished with archaeological finds. With the ramp, sharp turns around the twisted hoardings, and its music, the second section was visceral, almost disorienting (Basu & Macdonald 2007, 15–6). Although, even in the first part of the exhibition, one video featured the principal archaeologist waxing lyrical about boyhood dreams of exploration and the thrill of standing among the ruins themselves, the juxtaposition of the 'disaster scene' and – 'removing temporal references' (Albano 2018, 105) – the exhibits and accounts of methodology amongst the cool scaffolding could not have made it clearer that there are different ways to assess the evidence for history or archaeology. The contrast between the anastylotic arrangement of Marcus Aurelius's fragments at the start and the horizontal array of Hadrian's at the end implied the same point: interpretation is a process of contemporary judgement.

There was even a little prompt to that effect in the second section: half hidden behind one of the leaning walls as if left carelessly by the designer, lay a little pile of tubes in the set's principal colours. Considering that the spectacular 'disaster scene' could have distracted from the exhibition's general purpose, that was quite a confident trick of distancing (*sensu* Bertolt Brecht), exposing the museological artifice. Shown likewise were some of the crates in which the exhibits had arrived from Turkey: we gather what we select as evidence for the past, they suggested; and our interpretations of those finds are constructs.

The Sainsbury Centre made the same point more explicitly. The corridor between the exhibition's two parts functioned like the central passages in *Sagalassos* but it was blank. Rather than drawing us into a 'dream', it interrupted our 'flow' before the second part of the exhibition pulled us back from the past. Where the first part spotlit the ancient figurines in a comparatively simple lay-out, the second offered a bright and busy range of suggestive hints about meaning or significance. Without seeing the second part first, the effect of the corridor can only have been subliminal. The second part then more or less told us to take the responsibility for interpretation. Andrew Cochrane's contributions were evidently intended to reinforce the invitation by punctuating our flow.

Results

The five exhibitions balanced familiarity and novelty in various ways. For *Watertight*, *Poriveski Kõrts* and *Krieg*, the task was to interest us in things or activities more or less familiar. The figurines in *Unearthed*, to the contrary, looked weird, while, for *Sagalassos*, one challenge must have been to evoke for Belgians, so innocent of the experience, the impact of a severe earthquake.

Whether or not because their respective topics, in such different ways, were defined more simply, *Kõrts* and *Krieg* were conceptually and interpretively less complicated than the other three. Where the former depended on immersion, *Krieg* tried to engage us by stirring empathy. Perhaps for the same reason, cheerful and dismal respectively, these two exhibitions were at the poles of the spectrum of tone where the others depended on drawing us through an intermediate range of moods.

To provoke thought, it was suggested, above, requires three basic factors: curiousness, a question or message, and design. Consider, then, for the sake of argument, the assessments in Table 6.1. *Watertight Sources* provided explicit texts in a conventional design. The interpretation was simple but somewhat open-ended. It was simpler still in *Kõrts*, but that exhibition depended on a surprising design to encourage thought about comparatively familiar items. *Sagalassos*, with less familiar exhibits, sought to convey its principal messages by means of a very unusual design. Yet, if the intense spaces, there, were the most memorable as spaces, *Krieg*'s plainer presentation was, in Tilden's sense, the most 'disturbing'. Its impact sprang less from the exhibits in themselves, most of which were familiar in appearance, than from its long, insistent sequence of evidence for warfare. *Unearthed* presented both very familiar things and strange ones. In seeking to draw us into participation through

Table 6.1: Familiarity of the exhibitions' fundamental features

Familiarity	Exhibits	Question	Design
most	Kõrts	Kõrts	Watertight
more	Watertight	Watertight	Krieg
	Krieg	Krieg	Kõrts
less	Sagalassos	Sagalassos	Unearthed
least	Unearthed	Unearthed	Sagalassos

its lay-out and by eliciting interpretation both through the example of the previous visitors' models and by inviting us directly, *Unearthed* was the most open-ended and radical exhibition.

Sagalassos and *Watertight* presented finds as cultural assets or resources in Carman's sense. Then, where *Sagalassos* proceeded from the archaeological record of the ancient world into the 'disaster scene' as a humanistic evocation and back to finds as the basis for the record, *Unearthed* led us from the ancient figurines, as a resource, to consider archaeology not only as remains from the past but also as heritage. At the time, *Sagalassos* may have implied a political issue about contemporary Belgium but the figurines in *Unearthed* were presented quite plainly as images for thinking about gender in general and then about authority too and, by extension, about the structure of a whole way of life, ours as well as the ancients'. It was not just that the Sainsbury Centre is an art gallery, for, like *Sagalassos*, *Unearthed* described scientific assessment alongside an approach through the humanities.

Both exhibitions showed how a corridor prompts, literally, a different footing. In *Unearthed*, that allowed us to refresh our concentration while, in *Sagalassos*, the space was used to intrigue us with its enigmatic words and a vague glimpse of the scene to follow; but both corridors also let the design recover some of the initiative from us. The low door into the pub scene had the same function but, partly because *Kõrts* was so small, the interruption was less marked. In contrast, *Krieg* and *Watertight* counted more on content for effect than on form.

Could Gardner's principle of 'intelligences' help to show how the exhibitions tried to engage us? Consider Table 6.2, for the sake, again, of argument. All five, of course, showed finds and supplementary displays. Only *Kõrts* dispensed with reading. Immersing us, both *Kõrts* and *Sagalassos* used musical rhythm to suggest mood; and *Sagalassos* in particular required environmental and kinetic alertness. *Kõrts* dispensed completely with words but the board game invited counting. As usual, none of the exhibitions necessarily required social skills (although some cooperation was needed among so many wrapt visitors in *Sagalassos*). There were elements to unsettle us in each but only *Unearthed* directly prompted awareness of our own evaluations.

Table 6.2: 'Intelligences' for the exhibitions (Davis et al. 2011)

Intelligence	Watertight	Kõrts	Unearthed	Sagalassos	Krieg
visual	•	•	•	•	•
environment		•	(•)	•	
kinetic		•		•	
rhythm		•		•	
verbal	•		•	•	•
logic, counting		•			
social					
self			•		

Must critical thinking be confined to universities? Self-awareness is needed for anyone legitimately to take part in interpretation anywhere; and then we may find, as Tilden anticipated, that issues follow us out of any gallery.

Acknowledgements

I thank Lucilla Burn for her encouragement, Dr Gaskell for showing me his critique, Dr Christophilopoulou for letting me adapt my contribution to the meeting and John Goldsmith for commenting on a draft of the result. The editors sending me to such stimulating exhibitions were Martin Carver and Chris Scarre.

References

Albano, C. (2018) The Exhibition as an Experiment: An Analogy and its Implications. *Journal of Visual Culture* 17, 97–116.

Bailey, D., Cochrane, A. & Zambelli, J. (2010) *Unearthed: A Comparative Study of Jōmon Dogū and Neolithic Figurines.* n.p., Norwich, Sainsbury Institute for the Study of Japanese Art & Culture.

Basu, P. & Macdonald, S. (2007) Introduction: Experiments in Exhibitions, Ethnography, Art, and Science. In S. Macdonald & P. Basu (eds), *Exhibition Experiments*, 1–24. Malden, Blackwell.

Black, G. (2005) *The Engaging Museum: Developing Museums for Visitor Involvement.* Abingdon, Routledge.

Burn, L. (2016) *The Fitzwilliam Museum: A History.* London, Philip Wilson.

Carman, J. (2002) *Archaeology and heritage: an introduction.* London, Continuum.

Cochrane, A. & Russell, I. (2007) Visualizing Archaeologies: A Manifesto. *Cambridge Archaeological Journal* 17, 3–19.

Davis K., Christodoulou J., Seider S. & Gardner, H. (2011) The Theory of Multiple Intelligences. In R. J. Sternberg & S. B. Kaufman (eds), *Handbook of Intelligence*, 485–503. Cambridge, Cambridge University Press.

Gaskell, I. (2016) *Krieg: eine archäologische Spurensuche.* West 86th, 7 June http://www.west86th.bgc. bard.edu/notes-from-the-filed/ [sic] (accessed August 2016).

Hooper-Greenhill, E. (1994) *Museums and Their Visitors.* London, Routledge.

James, N. (2012) The Romans: Dream or Nightmare? *Antiquity* 86, 1210–5.

James, N. (2013) Resource and Interpretation. *Antiquity* 87, 270–6.

James, N. (2016) 'Hot Interpretation' of Battle. *Antiquity* 90, 1100–3.

James, N. & Chippindale, J. (2010) Figurine Enigmas: Who's to Know? *Antiquity* 84, 1172–6.

King, L. & Marstine, J. (2006) The University Museum and Gallery: A Site for Institutional Critique and a Focus of the Curriculum. In J. Marstine (ed.), *New Museum Theory and Practice*, 266–91. Malden, Blackwell.

Shanks, M. & Tilley C. (1992) *Re-constructing Archaeology: Theory and Practice* (2nd ed.). London, Routledge.

Swain, H. (2007) *An Introduction to Museum Archaeology.* Cambridge, Cambridge University Press.

Tilden, F. (1977) *Interpreting our Heritage* (3rd ed.). Chapel Hill, NC, University of North Carolina Press.

Unearthed Team (2010) *Unearthed.* Norwich, Sainsbury Centre for Visual Arts.

Uzzell, D. L. (1989) The Hot Interpretation of War and Conflict. In D. L. Uzzell (ed.), *Heritage Interpretation*, 1, 33–47. London, Belhaven.

Chapter 7

Re-inventing Public Archaeology in Greece

Nena Galanidou

Introduction

Archaeology has always fascinated people, with the captivating tension contained in historicised memories and the cultural past, and with the explosive ambiguity of its doubts and certainties. Its great power rests in the materiality of its finds, which originate from antiquity, tangible things that everyone can appreciate. This power is multiplied when it meets the existential human quest for identity and roots. This is why the heart of archaeology has always beaten in the present. The theoretical starting-points, questions, definitions, interpretations and narratives may depart from the archaeological universe but, in the real world of economic conflict and political struggle, they reach far further. In this study, I address how the public is engaged with the past brought to light by archaeology in Greece. Here sites and monuments are omnipresent, both physically in the landscape and the cityscape, and metaphorically as a symbolic entity in the landscape of identity. I explore the intricate relationship between the official bodies of archaeology and the public and the conditions under which this relationship is reshaped and transformed. Official archaeology in Greece has traditionally approached Public Archaeology's mission as one of knowledge dissemination, education and communication, recording an impressive output on this front (for instance see Eleftheriou *et al.*, Lagogianni-Georgakarakos *et al.* and Klonizaki in this volume; Soueref 2018). My aim is to examine two recent initiatives in Public Archaeology that have a different point of departure, mobilising civil society and forging a novel, participatory and more inclusive approach to archaeological heritage protection. They readdress the interactions and power relations between the material culture of the past, groups and individuals.

From Archaeology and the Public or Archaeology for the Public to Public Archaeology

There is an interactive process and a dialectic relationship between the archaeologist, the archaeological evidence and the public, that is the citizens' body that constitutes public opinion (Habermas 1962; Melton 2001). This process scientifically and experientially defines and shapes Public Archaeology, in its core conceptualisation. Within this frame, Public Archaeology is the vehicle conveying scientific research to the public; its primary mission is to act as an intermediary, making archaeology familiar and accessible to all. In a magical and deterministic way, a large part of archaeology escapes from the excavation trenches, the laboratories and the specialist journals or conferences, the fora where archaeological science is produced and touches the public sphere, by which it is reproduced. Public Archaeology is also in a constant dialogic relationship with the zeitgeist, even being privileged, occasionally, to create it. The interpretations, the stresses, the suppressions and underlining that convey the thread from archaeology to the public sphere and vice versa, often converge with critical national and political issues at the forefront of public opinion. Public Archaeology is thus capable of founding or undermining group memory and identity, whether national or local.

In the last decades of the 20th century, a distinct sub-field of scientific specialisation arose, with its own subject matter and its own methodology, under the general title of Public Archaeology. The publication by McGimsey (1972) was the ideal starting-point of what was, for the first time, named Public Archaeology: an archaeology that pursues active public participation in the protection of monuments and cultural heritage, utilising education, knowledge and participation. Since then, the intellectual fruits of Public Archaeology have gradually ripened, in the form of conferences, monographs, printed and digital journals, university courses, curricula and doctoral dissertations.

The main landmarks along this road, which started earlier – in fact prior to the coining of the term – with the first, strongly politicised World Archaeology Conference (WAC), held in Southampton in 1968 (Ucko 1987; Gero 2009), are: the 1999 thematic issue of the *European Journal of Archaeology*, with an editorial by Schadla-Hall, who defines Public Archaeology 'as any area of archaeological activity that interacted or had the potential to interact with the public' (1999, 147) and other relevant papers; the Public Archaeology MA course offered by UCL Institute of Archaeology since 1999; the launching of the *Public Archaeology* journal with an editorial by Ascherson (2000); the collective volume *Public Archaeology* edited by Merriman (2004a), originating from a session in the 1999 WAC in Cape Town; the European Association of Archaeologists Public Archaeology Working Group, established in 2013 as a network of professionals to work on both the refinement of Public Archaeology definition and the exchange of best practice examples (Richardson & Almansa-Sánchez 2015); and the publication of the proceedings of the *Sharing Archaeology* conference (Stone & Zhao 2015), where writing in a style suited to the different audiences of archaeology is deftly spelled out as an obligation rather than a choice (Stone 2015).

A creative polysemy is at play in the definition of Public Archaeology (see also discussion in Merriman 2004b; Carman 2002). According to Richardson and Almansa-Sánchez, Public Archaeology 'can be defined both as a disciplinary practice and as a theoretical position, which can be exercised through the democratization of archaeological communication, activity or administration, through communication with the public, the involvement of the public or the preservation and administration of archaeological resources for the public benefit by voluntary or statutory organisations' (2015, 195). It follows that, as a group of theories, methods and practices, Public Archaeology inspires and mobilises the whole range of the archaeological process. Conversely, the reception of archaeological activity by the public sphere and their interaction are also objects of Public Archaeology. In short, and very much like tango, it takes two to Public Archaeology. Archaeologists, museum people and all who play a part in the process of obtaining, interpreting, protecting, conserving, restoring, exhibiting and promoting archaeological remains are inextricably and actively paired with the public, which embraces, internalises, adopts or rejects the archaeology, exploits it financially or ideologically, creates myths and beliefs out of it, or merely deconstructs it.

A flexible definition of Public Archaeology addressing the polysemy of the term is that of *archaeology in the public sphere*. Within this definition, Public Archaeology embraces and handles a wide range of subjects, which arise both where archaeology intersects with and penetrates the public sphere, and where it is permeated by it. Both the public sphere and archaeology are context-specific and historically defined.

Beyond its core definition, Public Archaeology has received many alternative and at times, complementary treatments. Merriman (2004b) identifies two models. The *deficit model* stresses the importance of experts in encouraging better public understanding of the science of archaeology, both for its economic value and for the benefits it offers to citizens. This model recognises the importance of agency where archaeology meets the public sphere, as well as the need for the public to come to grips with certain essential values and principles of archaeology. The *multiple perspectives model* proposes that archaeological finds could be used by archaeologists to engage with the public, with the ultimate aim of enriching people's lives to stimulate thought, emotion and creativity.

Holtorf, in his thoughtful work *Archaeology is a Brand* (2007), elaborates on the relationship between science and society and identifies three competing yet non-mutually exclusive ways to approach public archaeology, ultimately deriving from different political philosophies. The *education model* asserts that archaeologists must help familiarise the public with both the past and the archaeologist's profession in the same terms as professional archaeologists themselves. It is an elitist approach that grants the monopoly on truth to the scientific side alone. The *public relations model* asserts that an increase in social, economic and political support for professional archaeologists will only be forthcoming if archaeologists improve the public image of their research activities. (Archaeological) science is one of many players in the public arena and, its presence and authority can only solidify through integrated interaction and dialogue with the public. At the opposite pole to these two models, which treat the public as a passive recipient of archaeological achievement, the *democratic model* is in line with an open and democratic science that works to restore society's trust in it. This model suggests that everyone, regardless of education, profession or training, can develop their enthusiasm and interest in archaeology. Archaeology needs to move beyond either acting as a gatekeeper of the past or branding itself as the sole authority permitted to make plans relating to the material culture of the past. Instead, it must engage with the people, local or indigenous, in working cooperatively on heritage management or archaeological projects (Broadbent 2004; Holtorf 2007, 119–21). The model treats non-scientists as potential active participants in the archaeological process and interpretation and relies on the rules of democracy to operate as a problem mitigation strategy. The first two models approach the public as people, ignorant and incompetent to make valid judgements about science and reality without archaeological agency, whereas the third model approaches the public as citizens, with the critical capacity to judge maturely and thus to be part of archaeological agency.

The Greek Experience of Public Engagement with the Archaeological World

Official archaeology in Greece forms part of the public sector and rests on two pillars: I. the Antiquities Service (AS) and II. academics and researchers working in universities and research institutes. The former is the state-appointed administrative body in charge of archaeological heritage management (research, conservation, restoration, protection, exhibition and promotion). Founded in 1833, it was originally part of the Ministry of Religious and Public Education to excavate and preserve acquisitions and to prevent the illegal export of antiquities (Kokkou 1977; Mpihta 2008, 23). Today it operates at prefectural and national level under the Ministry of Culture and Sports. The second pillar is formed of the employees of the Ministry of Education, Research and Religious Affairs. They are responsible for teaching archaeology, providing expert consultancy to state councils, conducting research and, intermittently, training professional tourist guides (Galanidou 2012). In 2012–14 they formed one-tenth of the total of employees in the Antiquities Service (https://www.discovering-archaeologists.eu/national_reports, table 1).

The enactment of laws regulating the relationship of archaeology to and its integration into the social and economic process, based on the protection of monuments and cultural heritage, has played a catalytic role in the integration of archaeology in the public sphere. In Greece, as early as 1830 the Administrative Circular 953 drawn up by Andreas Moustoxydis (Kokkou 1977; Haralambides 2008), and a little earlier or later in other countries (*e.g.* 1802 in Italy and 1882 in the UK), expressed the demand of knowledgeable and educated legislators that antiquities should be respected and protected from damage, destruction and looting in order to hand them down to future generations. Almost two centuries later, official archaeology in Greece is now armed with a constitutional and legal framework that explicitly spells out its mission and operation. The archaeological law of 2002 classifies work in the field as either 'salvage' or 'systematic'. Salvage work can only be conducted by the employees of the AS. Systematic work comprises large-scale, long-term projects that, besides archaeologists working for the AS, can also be conducted by Greek and foreign academics or researchers – the latter on condition that they are attached to one of the foreign schools of archaeology operating in Greece and only under the supervision of the AS. The state is responsible for archaeological heritage and any archaeological activity, no matter who is directing or funding it requires the permission of the Culture Minister.

The early 20th century witnessed an attempt of the utmost importance to conceptually and ideologically define the canon and refine the priorities of archaeology in Greece. The International Archaeology Conference held in Athens in 1905 was a landmark in this process (Alexandri 2008). Until the late 1960s, official archaeology had established its authority to set the rules of excavation, curation and protection of antiquities in Greece. Its institutional mechanisms gave rise to a protected authenticity area, a symbolic and literal barrier to the reception of and access to the archaeological past. The spatial delimitation and fencing off of archaeological sites and monuments, or the museum displays that permitted visitors only visual contact with the exhibits, served the authentication, protection and exhibition of antiquities. By rendering visible the remains of the past, they underscored their importance in the present, filtered through the expert eye. Monitoring the citizens' encounter with the past was achieved by various means. A token of this is the standard closing paragraph of any archaeological permit to conduct systematic research: 'In order for research results to be announced in the media or on the internet, information must first be provided in writing to the Ephorate of Antiquities and the General Directorate of Antiquities and Cultural Heritage, accompanied by indicative visual material.'

In the last 30 years of the 20th century as the urban and tourist development, coupled with large-scale public and private construction work, put immense pressure on the natural and archaeological heritage of Greece, the concepts of 'authority' and 'authenticity' reached their peak. In 1971 the Ministry of Culture and Sciences was established, formed by the General Directorate of Cultural Affairs and the Directorate of Antiquities and Restoration (https://www.culture.gr/el/ministry/SitePages/history.aspx). The legal framework granting the AS the scientific authority to define and protect sites and monuments, coupled with the continuation and reproduction of a firmly hierarchical public administration, allowed the AS to fulfil its primary mission and, as a side effect, also save the natural setting of archaeological sites. Yet it alienated many potential partners, not only from other branches of the public sector but also from the private and civil sectors. In parallel, as democratic rules of governance were established and more stakeholders were introduced to the public scene, mostly narratives about the past produced in the context of official archaeology were considered, as opposed to local, indigenous, collective, tourist, commercial or literary narratives about the same past.[1]

Archaeology in Greece essentially remains a closed profession which has lacked, for reasons of political patronage, a steady influx of scientists selected based on unified criteria (https://www.discovering-archaeologists.eu/national_reports). Insufficient staffing has had detrimental effects on the speedy processing of citizens' cases and the effective protection of the monuments. The division of the AS into two different local Ephorates (one of Ancient and one of Modern Heritage), means that in some cases citizens are required to run the same bureaucratic gauntlet twice in an attempt, for example, to obtain a demolition permit if the building, or its ruins, is located atop both a Byzantine and a 19th-century monument. As a result, the public is often wary of archaeology. For many Greeks, archaeology is synonymous with bureaucratic difficulties and delays in everyday life, despite all they learned in school or the wonderful finds occasionally showcased by the media.

At the dawn of the 21st century there was a large gap at the point where archaeological science meets the public. This was due to the historical rift between the official archaeology and anyone outside it. The obvious pressures exerted on sites and monuments, both by politico-economic factors and by ordinary citizens, under the convenient guise of public development or personal prosperity, had turned archaeologists into saviours of sites and monuments and enemies of the people. But this heroism during a crisis of values came at a cost. In its attempt to defend itself, the AS had erected walls of introversion. The peril of heritage destruction had given rise to the equally perilous attitude of heritage possession.[2] Through this attitude, the AS secured the ideological and ethical apparatus to produce and reproduce itself and maintain its status. Yet it became socially ostracised. This ostracism may be understood as the ultimate defensive weapon against a society greedy to trample the rules underfoot in the name of development, collective and individual.

This rift between official archaeology and the public has not escaped the magnifying lens of Konstantios (2003), Labrinoudakis (2008) and Themelis (2015), who articulate a non-mainstream vision of cultural heritage protection. These three precious volumes of collected essays contain a wealth of ideas, initiatives and legislative changes required to demolish the wall that separates archaeology from its stakeholders. It is no coincidence that all three authors originally addressed the wider public, not only their peers, publishing their work in magazines and newspapers or making oral presentations.

The dominant view of Public Archaeology in Greece was that this is solely entrusted with conveying to the public the scientific and experiential knowledge acquired through archaeological work, from the expert, to the non-expert. While individual archaeologists of the AS worked together with the public to fulfil the aims of archaeology, the agenda of Public Archaeology was identified as knowledge dissemination;

this was the *raison d'être* of archaeological museum exhibitions and educational programmes. This approach fits well with Merriman's deficit model (2004) or Holtorf's education and public relations models (2007).

Public Archaeology in Greek Universities

Public Archaeology has also remained low on the list of educational and research priorities of Greek universities, where archaeology is taught and reproduced. Although it is taught as a seminar and as a course in the University of Crete, Public Archaeology still seems, at first glance, to be outside the core subjects of the other three Departments of History and Archaeology, which bear the chief burden of archaeological education within the Schools of Philosophy. In these departments the chronological breakdown into Prehistoric, Classical and Byzantine Archaeology and the focus on monuments and artefacts form the backbone of archaeological studies, which are supplemented by lectures in History, Art History and Literature. Demands for renewal and innovation in Archaeology curricula have only begun to be diffidently expressed in recent years, with proclamations of new, thematically specialised teaching and research staff positions. Courses in Museology are offered, limited to fruitful collaborations, *e.g.* between Archaeology, Architecture and Cultural Resources Management, but only in the context of interdepartmental and interuniversity postgraduate curricula. Schools of Philosophy apart, if we include in our discussion the three new departments in the service of archaeology – at the Universities of Thessaly, the Peloponnese and the Aegean – we observe that substantially different Archaeology curricula to those of the Schools of Philosophy are articulated. Students are taught, among other things, Museology and Cultural Resource Management. The time is ripe for Public Archaeology to become an organic part of archaeological education in undergraduate and postgraduate curricula. Archaeologists, responding to the needs and interests of modern society, must be taught about Public Archaeology in a systematic and coordinated way, absorbing elements of the international and Greek experience. One cannot expect professional attitudes to Public Archaeology to change unless we pave the way to this change, starting from archaeological education.

In 2013 the launch of a series by Kaleidoscope Editions, Athens, intended to harness Public Archaeology in Greek language, was an academic initiative in tune with the broader effort to bring the archaeological community into contact with its multifaceted and multivalent audience while remaining in step with international attempts to provide a systematic scientific approach to all the elements that make up Public Archaeology. The editors intend to host original studies by Greek and international authors on the convergence and conversation between archaeology and the non-expert. We hope that the series will form an active part of the Greek contribution to the cultivation of Public Archaeology and a teaching tool for Public Archaeology in Greek universities.[3]

Re-inventing Public Archaeology

For almost two centuries, the task of site and monument management and their protection has been undertaken by the Greek public sector through the delimitation and
monitoring of the archaeological past. Such an approach does not entail but benefits
from the involvement and assistance of ordinary people and stakeholders. Many different voices, both from the official archaeology and outside it, are making a case for
revising the roadmap for the protection of the archaeological heritage. Simply put,
citizen empowerment is emerging as a further tool in reinforcing monitoring. In this
section, I examine two recent initiatives that have sprung from the academic world
and the civil sector to articulate a new approach to archaeology in the public sphere.

The first initiative flags the importance of empowering a local community to
engage with its Palaeolithic heritage. Every summer since 2012, the University of
Crete has conducted systematic excavations at the half a million-year-old site at
Lisvori – Rodafnidia on the island of Lesbos. This is the first Lower Palaeolithic site
in Greece to yield compelling evidence for the presence of hominins using Acheulean
technology (Galanidou *et al.* 2013; 2016). It is situated on a spur of a low hill, where
a large olive grove, segmented into numerous properties, extends today. The site is
extensive, and the team has made the deliberate choice to explore different parts
of it by digging only in those fields whose owners grant permission. The people's
consensus to authorise excavation is deemed a prerequisite to research. A total of
35 archaeological trenches have thus far been explored in 21 properties owned by
people living in the nearby villages. At the end of each field season we backfill the
trenches and we return the fields to their owners to carry on with the agricultural
activity. The archaeological work has been incorporated in the annual cycle of village
life. Excavation and surface survey take place in the very same place where agricultural work is conducted, complementing rather than replacing each other. When the
fieldwork began in 2012 the team encountered mixed feelings of hostility or indif-
ference by the locals. The research objective and requirements of the project were
indifferent to the small and elderly agricultural community. The Greek public views
archaeology with an attitude of subversion and a fear of loss or freezing of property
and the project was conducted by non-locals, members of a far-flung university. Over
the years, the team's all-inclusive approach to the community has addressed these
reservations and brought about a remarkable shift in a different attitude.

The public programme embraces the village people, the immediate neighbours and
the islanders of Lesbos, both those living on Lesbos and in Athens, and is structured
in two phases. During each field season, citizens of all ages and backgrounds – from
school children to local fishermen, medical doctors, tourists or clergy (Fig. 7.1) – are
encouraged to visit and, when possible, participate in the excavation, supervised by a
senior team member. The head of the village council is encouraged to be daily present
in the trenches to oversee the progress of work and help carry or maintain the excavation equipment, given that the excavation team consists solely of archaeologists
and students and does not employ any workmen. Every evening the archaeology lab

Figure 7.1: The clergy of Lesbos engaging with the Palaeolithic heritage and the University of Crete field crew at a Lisvori - Rodafnidia trench in summer 2015 (image: Nena Galanidou/University of Crete).

housed in the local primary school is open to anyone interested in seeing the yield of the day, helping to wash finds or simply wanting a friendly chat. Those who come to the lab obtain hands-on experience of Palaeolithic artefacts and are encouraged to bring in objects found in the fields when the archaeological team is absent. Every time the team returns to Lisvori, stone objects with potential archaeological value collected by locals are submitted for evaluation. Where these proved to be artefacts rather than natural rocks, the citizens are praised and given further information on their finds. In this way, they become active participants in the archaeological discovery and provide valuable information on unknown sites. Before closing the trenches there is an annual open meeting with the local community to share the results of the fieldwork and answer questions (Fig. 7.2). This is an event that unites the different gender and age groups of the community whose public space is spatially differentiated. These meetings function as a social and cultural platform for both sides, archaeologists and locals, to exchange views and feelings (*sensu* Fan 2015, 186), alleviate tensions and confrontation, openly discuss problems encountered by the team and plan fundraising or communication strategies.

Figure 7.2: Lisvori – Rodafnidia: A member of the archaeological team encourages visitors to have a hands-on experience of Palaeolithic large cutting tools in the laboratory. The laboratory is housed in the Lisvori primary school which is now closed; the archaeologists stay and work in it during the field expeditions every spring and summer (image: Nena Galanidou/ University of Crete).

Once the fieldwork is over, the communication thread is maintained through press-releases in the local and national press, TEDx presentations, radio and television interviews and oral presentations of the findings at Lesbos Association gatherings in Athens. Senior team members share the canon of their discipline as well as the uncertainties and difficulties encountered during research in the field. The members of the community respond by taking an active part in this archaeological journey, seeing the finds as part of their own identity and heritage. They now share with the archaeological team the anthropocentric and ecumenical view of the past unveiled by Palaeolithic archaeology (Galanidou 2008). They often envision handaxes as the smartphones of prehistoric people, multi-purpose tools that fit in one's hand and contain the technological achievements of half a million years ago. The archaeological narrative about the Palaeolithic dispersals to Lesbos is also a means of linking the past with the present. In recent years, due to its close proximity to the Anatolian coast, Lesbos has assumed the significant burden of the refugee and immigrant wave after the Syrian war. The archaeological narrative that the findings at Lisvori – Rodafnidia are a testimony to the origins and roots of human migration in this part of the world helps place the recent wave in a deep historical perspective.

As a result of this public programme a relationship of mutual trust has been established. The local community not only welcome the archaeological team, providing accommodation in their homes, but people even ask why excavations have not yet been conducted on their own properties. The community has gained respect for its own heritage through physical interaction with the site, the finds and the working team. Archaeologists and locals share the dream of giving Lisvori – Rodafnidia a brand name and turning it into a place that will keep its young people at home, allowing them a dignified life by means of a sustainable economy. They share the vision of turning the village's old oil-press into a Palaeolithic heritage information centre to complement the outdoor visit to the site. This dual destination scheme is expected to attract visitors and act as a core of local economic and cultural identity. It will also boost the primary sector, which includes small-scale yields of high-quality chickpea, onion, wheat, anise, cumin, sardines and salt. This interaction has helped the academic team, teachers and students alike, to realise the imperative need for archaeologists to gain exposure as a community through their multifaceted meeting with society, and to transform their peculiar introversion into a social and public good; to experience the liberating osmosis of the fascinating archaeological adventure together with society. Engagement with the public, *i.e.* the local communities of Lesbos, is not a research priority but a genetic trait of the University of Crete work.

The second initiative is Diazoma, a non-profit, non-governmental association working for the preservation and maintenance of Ancient Greek theatres. Inspired and run by former Greek Culture Minister Stavros Benos, it was founded by a group of intellectuals, scholars, artists and academics in 2008 (Fig. 7.3). Among the founding members were Vassilis Lambrinoudakis and Petros Themelis professors emeriti in Classical Archaeology who, as we saw earlier, had openly expressed their vision of establishing a closer bond between the archaeological heritage and the public in Greece (Lambrinoudakis 2008; Themelis 2015) (Fig. 7.4). Today, people in local government, proactive citizens and corporate members of the Greek business community also embrace Diazoma. In its 12 years of life it has been successful in raising funds for the research, study, protection, enhancement and, wherever feasible, the use of ancient theatres and other venues, such as ancient odeia and stadia, for performances and music events, art exhibitions and educational activities. The people involved in Diazoma work together, as helpers and supporters of the state and the services responsible, in the major task of including ancient monuments in modern social, intellectual and economic life (http://www.diazoma.gr/en/our-mission/). According to its founder, 'Diazoma aspires to be a model association in the way it functions, in the transparency of its economic management, the effectiveness of its actions, the achievement of its goals. Our aim is not to find, nor simply to persuade, but to inspire the big sponsors, to assist the services responsible, to mobilize the Ministry of Culture, to draw more and more of our fellow-citizens along with us in our work.' (http://www.diazoma.gr/en/our-mission/).

The ideological precepts and the organisational tools to achieve the coming together of monuments, nature and culture with real life and people throughout their full range of activities are *universal protection* as an ideological arsenal and *synergy* as a programmatic philosophy and process. Universal protection is summarised in the

Figure 7.3: The president of Diazoma, Stavros Benos (foreground), with Diazoma members and friends at the Mikrothives ancient theatre, Thessaly (image: Nena Galanidou).

motto 'monuments do not live, do not breathe, do not exist without human care and engagement'. By exploiting the results of synergy between citizens, institutions, local and prefectural authorities, sponsors and European funding schemes, Diazoma plans and proposes the implementation of new programs, whose aim is on the one hand the monuments' maintenance and restoration, on the other hand their connection with sustainability and sustainable development. These programmes, known as *Cultural Itineraries & Archaeological Parks*, are gradually expanding to almost all regions of Greece.

What is special about Diazoma is that not only does it provide new ways of bringing together ordinary people and archaeological heritage, but it does so in an innovative and holistic way, beyond the limits of state provision. The second major contribution of Diazoma is that it has challenged the perception that monuments are sacred places detached from contemporary society, and has helped bring them back into daily use for people in various cultural and educational activities. Through this path, it has raised public awareness of the archaeological heritage, while supporting contemporary artistic creation (see for instance Tuned City, Ancient Messene, 1–3 2018 https://www.youtube.com/watch?v=R9WIJEffMHQ).

Figure 7.4. The first general assembly of Diazoma in ancient Messene, Peloponnese in October 2008. The excavator of the site Petros Themelis and Stavros Benos talking to the participants (image: Nena Galanidou).

The third significant contribution of Diazoma is that, in its attempt to mobilise both citizens and state, it has clarified the concepts of the *state* in combination and association with the *public good*.

> The constitutional duty of the state may be to defend the monuments, but at the same time, the protection of the natural and cultural environment is everybody's "right" (Article 24 of the Greek Constitution). So, every citizen bears the state within himself or herself, is part of it both as an active citizen and as a producer. The Archaeological Law (Law 3028/2002, Article 3) states that the protection of the country's cultural heritage lies in – among other things – citizens' awareness. It follows that public and therefore cultural goods are not just state goods, as one might mistakenly suppose, based on a common identification of the public sector and the state; they are, by definition, public in the sense that has always permeated democratic thought and deed, institutionalised or otherwise: that of the citizen's personal right to and duty towards the public good. Those who believe that it is their duty, apart from using and experiencing the public good, also to contribute according to their capabilities, individually or collectively, to the protection and promotion of that good, will always be ideal citizens. (Benos pers. comm. 13.11.2008).

Discussion

Acknowledging that the protection of monuments is ensured through legislation and monitoring, but also through public awareness of their significance, the initiatives described above work towards securing the protection of Greece's archaeological heritage first and foremost by activating forces drawn from the civil sector. They have different genotypes, but their phenotype shares the view that the protection of archaeological heritage power cannot ignore civil society. They fall within Holtorf's *democratic model* of Public Archaeology and signal changes with profound effects in the relationship between official archaeology and the public in Greece. First and foremost, they reinvent Public Archaeology as an all-encompassing, dynamic process of interaction between the expert and the non-expert that develops over time. Secondly, they breathe new life into the fundamental mission and alliances of official archaeology. In effect, they work to change the socio-political power relations in the negotiation and implementation of archaeological practice and interpretation.

We have argued elsewhere that archaeology has never been an ivory tower, separate from the world, but a window on the great problems and questions facing humanity (Dommasnes & Galanidou 2007). Having recently emerged from a recession in which archaeologist unemployment reached its century peak, and as we are preparing for the next global crisis one due to the coronavirus pandemic, life is changing rapidly. Many traditional jobs are lost and will not be regained; wider political consensus is promoted to save the economy and the welfare state, e-learning platforms are widely used to maintain education, while Information Technology will speed up the fourth industrial revolution. What might be the future of official archaeology in Greece, in terms of the subjects, the people who serve it, and the objects, the role of antiquities in society and the economy? As a university teacher, I cannot but wonder what is the point of educating archaeology graduates and post-graduates if there are no archaeological jobs regularly available on the basis of a transparent selection procedure. What might be the future of antiquities and the museums that house them if they remain things to admire but 'not touch'? Okamura (2011) in line with theorists of cultural heritage management who claim that the value of cultural properties is contingent, questions the inherent value of archaeological objects and makes a strong case for communication and negotiation. He argues that (Japanese) society could attribute more meaning to archaeology if Public Archaeology shifted its emphasis from cultural properties, *i.e.* objects, to the public, *i.e.* the people (2011, 85).

Founded upon the principle of citizen empowerment, Diazoma and the University of Crete Palaeolithic Lesbos Project have carved a new path towards promoting a holistic view of the archaeological heritage in the 21st-century social and economic setting. Both have worked to achieve an advanced level of cooperation between official archaeology and the public, based on education, trust and a vision of sustainability. The members and friends of Diazoma and the people of Lesbos have tested the two initiatives and have chosen to work together to fulfil their aims and methods. Through these two initiatives, they have thus demystified archaeology sharing a new vision centred around sites and monuments, that could potentially help Greece protect its antiquities and fight poverty, especially during the impending recession. Archaeological heritage, natural environment and local economy, the three together form a unique resource around which new job opportunities could be created, and an alternative kind of development to building new hotels and cementing over the countryside could be offered. These initiatives contribute to the healthy and dynamic development of a reinvented Public Archaeology. It is no longer approached as synonymous with mere 'dissemination', but as 'participation', inclusive rather than exclusive. The large gap at the point where antiquities meet the public is gradually being filled, and a healthy interaction and engagement with the non-expert serves heritage and society rather than the reproduction of archaeology itself. Archaeology is approached as a source of knowledge on the human condition and culture, aesthetic pleasure and prosperity.

Notes

1 The history of the interaction of the AS with the public in the second half of the 20th century in Greece is the subject of systematic research conducted in the University of Crete post-doctorate and PhD programmes. Despoina Nazou works on 'Archaeology, Tourism and Island Communities: Perception, conceptualisation and appropriation of the archaeological record in island Greece', Ariadne Gazi examines 'Archaeology in Greece from the Civil War to the Period of Political Transition through the Archive of Stylianos Alexiou', and Georgia Beka examines 'Palaeolithic Heritage: Reception, perception and appropriation by the local communities of island and rural Greece'.
2 The possessive mentality is undoubtedly not only a Greek but a global phenomenon. Regarding the Chinese experience, Ling notes that, while archaeology is an academic discipline, it 'is not the exclusive property of archaeological experts, but is an integral part of the study of human culture' (2010, 51).
3 The first book, *Telling Children about the Past: An Interdisciplinary Perspective* (Galanidou & Dommasnes 2007), is a translation of the original published in Ann Arbor (now available through Berghahn Books). Interdisciplinary in character, it brings together knowledge and ideas produced in academic ecosystems in the USA, France, Greece, the UK, Norway, Brazil and Romania. After a gestation period coinciding with the economic crisis in Greece, the second book, entitled *Museum Sites in the Twenty-First Century: Practices of Interaction* was published in 2018 (Soueref 2018). In tune with Holtorf's democratic model (2007), the collective volume brings together archaeologists working in the AS to explore the fertile ground of interaction between the expert and the other rather than dissemination in a strict hierarchical expert – audience scheme.

References

Alexandri, A. (2008) Το πρώτο διεθνές αρχαιολογικό συνέδριο στην Ελλάδα. In M. Tsipopoulou (ed.) «...*Ανέφερα Εγγράφως» Θησαυροί του Ιστορικού Αρχείου της Αρχαιολογικής Υπηρεσίας*, 47–50. Thessaloniki, Ministry of Culture and Tourism, Archaeological Museum of Thessaloniki, National Archive of Monuments.

Ascherson, N. (2000) Editorial. *Public Archaeology* 1(1), 1–4.

Broadbent, N. D. (2004) Saami prehistory, identity and rights in Sweden. In *Proceedings of the Third Northern Research Forum: The Resilient North - Human Responses to Global Change*. https://www.rha.

is/static/files/NRF/OpenAssemblies/Yellowknife2004/3rd-nrf_plenary-3_broadbent_final.pdf (accessed 13 April 2020).

Carman, J. (2002) *Archaeology and Heritage: An Introduction.* London, New York, Continuum.

Dommasnes, L. H. & Galanidou, N. (2007) Introduction. Children and Narratives of the Past. In N. Galanidou & L.H. Dommasnes (eds) *Telling Children About the Past: An Interdisciplinary Perspective,* 1–16. Ann Arbor, MI, International Monographs in Prehistory.

Fan, J. (2015) How to Share Archaeological Excavation *in situ* with the Public: A Case Study from Nanwang Site in Shandong Province, China. In P. G. Stone & H. Zhao (eds) *Sharing Archaeology: Academe, Practice and the Public,* 180–98. New York, London, Routledge.

Galanidou, N. (2008) The Palaeolithic for Children: Text and Identity. In L.H. Dommasnes & M. Wrigglesworth (eds) *Children, Identity and the Past,* 181–205. Newcastle, Cambridge Scholars Publishing.

Galanidou, N. (2012) Προλεγόμενα στη Δημόσια Αρχαιολογία. In N. Galanidou, & L. H. Dommasnes (eds) *Μιλώντας στα Παιδιά για το Παρελθόν: - Μια Διεπιστημονική Προσέγγιση,* 11–20. Athens, Kaleidoskopio.

Galanidou, N. & Dommasnes L.H. (eds) (2007) *Telling Children about the Past: An Interdisciplinary Perspective.* Ann Arbor, MI, International Monographs in Prehistory.

Galanidou, N. & Dommasnes L. H. (eds) (2012) *Μιλώντας στα Παιδιά για το Παρελθόν.* Athens, Kaleidoskopio.

Galanidou, N., Cole, J., Iliopoulos, G. & McNabb, J. (2013) East meets West: The Middle Pleistocene Site of Rodafnidia on Lesvos, Greece. *Antiquity,* 87(336). https://www.antiquity.ac.uk/projgall/galanidou336/.

Galanidou, N., Athanassas, C., Cole, J., Iliopoulos, G., Katerinopoulos, A., Magganas, A. & McNabb, J. (2016) The Acheulian site at Rodafnidia, Lisvori, on Lesvos, Greece: 2010–2012. In K. Harvati & M. Roksandic (eds) *Paleoanthropology of the Balkans and Anatolia: Human Evolution and Its Context,* 119–38. Dordrecht, Springer.

Gero, J. (2009) *The History of World Archaeological Congress.* http://www.worldarchaeologicalcongress.org/about-wac/history/146-history-wac (accessed 14 April 2020).

Habermas, J. (1962) *The Structural Transformation of the Public Sphere. An Inquiry into a Category of Bourgeois Society* (trans. T. Burger & F. Lawrence 1989). Cambridge, Polity Press.

Haralambides, D. (2008) Θεσμοθέτηση και ίδρυση της Αρχαιολογικής Υπηρεσίας. In M. Tsipopoulou (ed.) *«...Ανέφερα Εγγράφως» Θησαυροί του Ιστορικού Αρχείου της Αρχαιολογικής Υπηρεσίας,* 13–17. Thessaloniki, Ministry of Culture and Tourism, Archaeological Museum of Thessaloniki, National Archive of Monuments.

Holtorf, C. (2007) *Archaeology is a Brand. The Meaning of Archaeology in Contemporary Popular Culture.* Walnut Creek, CA, Left Coast Press.

Kokkou, A. (1977) *Η Μέριμνα για τις Αρχαιότητες και τα Πρώτα Μουσεία.* Athens, Hermes.

Konstantios, D. (2003) *Η Πόλη, το Μουσείο, το Μνημείο. Δοκίμια πολιτιστικής διαχείρισης.* Athens, Scripta Publications.

Lambrinoudakis, V. (2008) *Οδοιπορικό από την Αρχαία Ελληνική Τέχνη στη Σύγχρονη Ζωή.* Athens, Eleuthero Panepistimio tis Stoas tou Vivliou – Livanis.

Ling, L. (2010) Sharing Archaeology with Whom? A Review of "Excavation Report of Hezhang-Kele Site in 2000'. In P. G. Stone & H. Zhao (eds) *Sharing Archaeology: Academe, Practice and the Public,* 47–56. New York, London, Routledge.

McGimsey, C. (1972) *Public Archaeology.* New York, Seminar Press.

Melton, J. V. H. (2001) *The Rise of the Public in Enlightenment Europe.* Cambridge, Cambridge University Press.

Merriman, N. (ed.) (2004a) *Public Archaeology.* London, Routledge.

Merriman, N. (2004b) Introduction: diversity and dissonance in public archaeology. In N. Merriman (ed.), *Public Archaeology,* 1–18. London, Routledge.

Mpichta, K. (2008) Το επίπονο έργο της αρχαιολογικής υπηρεσίας κατά τον 19ο αιώνα: περισυλλογή & καταγραφή τον αρχαιοτήτων. In M. Tsipopoulou (ed.) «...Ανέφερα Εγγράφως» Θησαυροί του Ιστορικού Αρχείου της Αρχαιολογικής Υπηρεσίας, 23–32. Thessaloniki, Ministry of Culture and Tourism, Archaeological Museum of Thessaloniki, National Archive of Monuments.

Okamura, K. (2011) From Object-centered to People-focused: Exploring a Gap Between Archaeologists and the Public in Contemporary Japan. In K. Okamura & A. Matsuda (eds) New Perspectives in Global Public Archaeology, 77–86. New York, Springer.

Richardson, L. J. & Almansa-Sánchez, J. (2015) Do You Even Know What Public Archaeology Is? Trends, Theory, Practice, Ethics. World Archaeology, 47(2), 194–211.

Schadla-Hall, T. (1999) Editorial: Public Archaeology. European Journal of Archaeology, 2(2), 147–58.

Soueref, K. (ed.) (2018) Μουσειακοί Χώροι στον Εικοστό Πρώτο Αιώνα: Πρακτικές Διάδρασης. Athens, Kaleidoskopio.

Stone, P. G. (2015) Sharing Archaeology: Introduction. In P. G. Stone & H. Zhao (eds.) Sharing Archaeology: Academe, Practice and the Public, 1–16. New York, London, Routledge.

Stone, P. G. & Zhao, H. (eds) (2015) Sharing Archaeology: Academe, Practice and the Public. New York, London, Routledge.

Themelis, P. (2015) Το Παρελθόν και το Σήμερα. Athens, Etaireia Messiniakon Archaiologikon Spoudon.

Ucko, P. (1987) Academic Freedom and Apartheid. The Story of the World Archaeological Congress. London, Duckworth.

Internet Resources

https://www.culture.gr/el/ministry/SitePages/history.aspx
http://www.diazoma.gr/en/our-mission/
https://www.discovering-archaeologists.eu/national_reports/2014/EL%20DISCO%202014%20Greece%20national%20report%20english%20.pdf
https://www.youtube.com/watch?v=R9WIJEffMHQ.

C. Voices from the Public: Audience and Community Driven Engagement within Museums

Chapter 8

Rendering the Public Visible in Curatorial Practice

Effrosyni Nomikou

Museum exhibitions conventionally embody the public engagement aspect of archaeology and related disciplines by affording a point of contact with the ancient world to the public. Yet, public engagement is still not necessarily considered as a core practice in the curatorial profession and even less so in the planning of permanent galleries. This chapter draws on a typical exhibition development story in a traditional Archaeology and Hhistory of Art museum, where a team of specialist curators put together a new permanent gallery, to make a point about the role and place of the public in curatorial exhibition practice. By pinning down a three-step process whereby the public becomes 'visible' and, consequently, a legitimate partner in exhibition development from conception until it opens, this chapter supports the argument that public engagement in museum practice should be regarded as a fundamental professional task rather than an add-on activity to the core curatorial remit.

The Shift Towards the Public

As documented by this volume, public engagement in museums with collections from the ancient world is enacted in many formats with varying degrees of commitment, reflexivity and success. This gradual – and long-awaited – shift in the relationship between museums with collections of the ancient world and their audiences is not a stand-alone development. The influences can be traced in at least two significant movements in relevant disciplines. On the one hand, there is the 'powerful momentum' of Public Archaeology, namely the 'practice and scholarship where archaeology meets the world', that has become most prevalent from the late 1990s onwards (Moshenska 2017b; see also Merriman 2004; Thomas & Lea 2014). Encompassing diverse forms of practice, from directly involving the public in archaeological investigations to community site management planning, and from museum programmes to popular culture memes; Public Archaeology is archaeology in inclusive mode, or at least with inclusive intentions. As the adjective 'public' is now standard in cultural heritage narratives (*e.g.* Labrador & Silberman 2018), 'the public', as a noun, is gaining recognition as a nuanced entity that comprises of individuals or groups of people with varied needs and interests.

Archaeology aside, a similar turn towards more participatory approaches is prevalent in other sectors of museological practice, notably in science, technology and natural history museums. These organisations deal with seemingly more topical issues that warrant public interest, in contrast to interpretations of the ancient world that do not seem to translate meaningfully into relevant discourses about the contemporary world. The museology of science museums has been engaging with the issue of public engagement far longer than have museums with collections from the ancient world. The trajectory of public engagement in the informal science sector is marked by educational theories and learning research that informs the ways science is presented to the public (see for example the large body of research on the CAISE platform (https://www.informalscience.org). On the same trajectory, we also find the influence of social movements and the challenge of the specialist to have shaped public engagement efforts (Moussouri 2014). Perhaps the most crucial development on that front has been the departure from a 'deficit model' that was presumed in 'public understanding of science' perspectives, towards more inclusive science communication practices that acknowledge heterogeneous publics as equal partners (Feinstein & Meshoulam 2014; Dawson 2018).

The surge in public engagement rhetoric and action, both in science and technology and the historical sciences, does not equate universal agreement about what public engagement entails. In the archaeological museum community, and among curators more specifically, the perceptions of what public engagement involves or ought to be, vary. Similarly, the range of practices that go under the umbrella-term of public engagement is wide. One-off programmes and add-on activities tend to outnumber organisation-wide strategies for effective engagement of the public. In some cases, public engagement is another term for outreach; namely, it takes place outside the museum. Often, public engagement initiatives question established curatorial norms and conflict with traditional museum practices (*e.g.* Hauptman Wahlgren & Svanberg 2008). Despite the differences, a common thread in all the definitions and approaches to participation/engagement is how far can the public be involved in the interpretations of the ancient world in a museum context (Moussouri 2014).

The shift towards more participatory practices in museums with collections from the ancient world that is the subject of this book can be situated in the above traditions. The wealth of public engagement research and experience, particularly in science communication, is an invaluable resource for museums with collections of the ancient world to tap on. A great deal of work has been done so that the public is given a voice and a platform to use it (Dawson 2018 and references therein). Drawing on these ideas, this chapter argues about the importance of rendering the public visible during exhibition development for a public engagement curatorial mindset to flourish.

Three Steps to Public Engagement

If we envisage a real turn in the practice of museums with collections from the ancient world with regards to public engagement, then the museum audience, the public, needs to be granted a more active role in the interpretations of the ancient world that are produced in these spaces. The public, with its nuanced identities, needs and characteristics, should be rendered as a visible partner in the meaning-making process involved in the production of narratives about antiquity. To this end, this chapter proposes a three-step procedure that can help guide museum practitioners towards more participatory exhibition practice. The proposed process is not meant to guarantee the blueprint to good public engagement. Instead, the three-step process is proposed here as an essential foundation to develop public engagement frame of mind among curators. The three steps described in this chapter show how public engagement becomes a curatorial mindset: one embedded in the professional agenda and carrying equal importance to other curatorial tasks.

Below, I explain each step of the process and, to illustrate my point, I use the case study from my doctoral research based on ethnographic data from the Ashmolean Museum redevelopment (Nomikou 2013). Dating back to 1683, the Ashmolean Museum of Art and Archaeology, home to the collections of the University of Oxford, is the oldest public museum in Britain. Between 2005 and 2009 it underwent a major transformation to make its historic collections more accessible to the public. The exhibition space was doubled with dozens of permanent galleries reconstructed and redesigned from scratch. The Heberden Coin Room, the Museum's Coins and Medals Department, one of the leading comprehensive collections in the world with some 300,000 items in its collection, partook in the Museum's transformation with the display of coins distributed across many of the new galleries, the setting up of a Study Room, a state of the art Coin Store and a flagship permanent Money Gallery. I followed the exhibition development closely, paying attention to the adaptation to and adoption of new museological practices, including more systematic public engagement attempts. Among other findings, I was able to explore the numismatic curators' perceptions of 'the public' as they were articulated and negotiated during the development of the permanent coin gallery. Audience consultation, a previously overlooked aspect of exhibition development in the Museum, came into play for the first time in the process and had a significant impact in the planning of the gallery.

Curatorial Assumptions about the Public

Curatorial assumptions about the public are central to exhibition decisions, even if these theories are not always made explicit. Essentially, the ideas curators have about the audience of their exhibition direct most decisions about the exhibition. This is not something new. The imagined public has always been a 'curatorially' constructed entity (Whitehead 2009). At the same time, the imagined public is not an exclusively curatorial construct, but a standard feature of communication, in fact any communication process. Research suggests that imagined audience alone can be just as influential as the actual audience in determining communication decisions and actions (Litt 2012). And while their influence is a given, these pre-existing ideas about visitors are often not clearly articulated, unless formally embedded in the development process. It is difficult to attain targets about public engagement if the expectations and convictions about the public are not communicated among the exhibition team in the first place. Thus, acknowledging and addressing the curatorial assumptions about the public is the fundamental first step towards translating these assumptions into good public engagement practice.

The imagined public tends to conform to a largely homogenised, standardised version of a visitor. It is straight-forward and convenient for curators to work with an abstract visitor profile in mind, one who displays coherent and predictable behaviour (Macdonald 2002). In my case study, the exhibition curators collectively imagined a specific version of the 'general public': that of a non-specialist individual with the reading age (and subsequent needs) of a 12-year-old person. They based this assumption mainly on the recommendation about the average reading age that was described in the *Text Housestyle Toolkit*. This tool was newly introduced in the exhibition practice of the museum at the time. Curators were advised to use it as guidance for writing labels and other gallery text. Having no specific direction about visitors at the beginning, and the perception that most people would not be familiar with (or interested in) specialist numismatic content, numismatic curators felt that a general comprehension level of a 12-year-old was a safe assumption. This form of 'visitor imagining', namely envisaging visitors as a non-subject specialist entity, is a common strategy that informs curatorial decisions as a standard. While this assumption is not strictly-speaking imprecise, it does little to overcome the 'us and them' divide (Macdonald 2002; Whitehead 2009). Instead, by informing curatorial decisions about exhibitions, the perpetual division between knowledgeable insiders and non-specialist outsiders hinders the possibility of meaningful public engagement. What is more, this division usually does not include non-visitors, *i.e.* the outsiders only refer to those who actually visit the museum, leaving a large segment of the public completely out of the museum agenda (Macdonald 2002; Dawson 2018).

Another common assumption about the prospective visitors to the Money Gallery was that of critical peers. When curators decided to expand the reach of the numismatic exhibition beyond the traditional audience, they expressed a certain nervousness about its reception from 'loyal', regular visitors. The more relaxed feel of the proposed new gallery could potentially put some visitors off. This prospect was carefully considered by curators, who felt they had to prepare for negative responses. It was a calculated risk that was taken because the curatorial team at the time felt confident about opening the exhibition's scope. In many cases, though, those 'imagined critics' may impede progressive ideas and direct curatorial decisions towards safer, traditional approaches (Macdonald 2002, 159).

The curators in my study said that when they prepared exhibits in the past, they had some ideas about prospective visitors that were more implicit than a distinct part of exhibition development. The difference this time was that these ideas, however arbitrary at the beginning, were vocalised and openly discussed. This was the result of formalised exhibition development process that required curatorial assumptions about visitors to be discussed with other specialist team members (museum educators, interpretation consultants and designers) who had been brought into the process. Vocalising curatorial assumptions about the public was the first step to render the public visible from an early stage in exhibition development, setting the foundations for a more inclusive exhibition practice.

Decisions Based on Evidence

Curatorial assumptions about the public need to be vocalised at an early stage of the exhibition development process so that they can be tested against evidence-based data about visitors. From conservation to ethical issues, curatorial best practice is about making informed rather than assumptions-based decisions about exhibitions. The issue of visitors should not be any different. However, the methodological scrutiny that naturally applies in other areas of curatorial practice is not necessarily present when it comes to including the public. If public engagement is to become an embedded curatorial practice in museums with collections from the ancient world, it should meet certain levels of methodological scrutiny. On this basis, curatorial assumptions about museum visitors and non-visitors need to be based on evidence to avoid futile stereotyping and bias. Moshenska highlights the need for a more systematic approach when public archaeologists (and by extension, in our case, museum curators) reach out to audiences:

> For a public-facing field, we know startlingly little about the public themselves: in any other industry, such a neglect of market research would have long ago proven terminal. This is not to say that public archaeologists have not surveyed and studied public attitudes and interests to archaeology, heritage and museums: there has been and continues to be fantastic work carried out in these areas worldwide. Rather, it is the lack of larger-scale studies or systematic meta-analyses that poses the problem: we might know a great deal about what the visitors to a specific museum enjoy, but we have few insights into the archaeological interests of the people of Norway or Tanzania on a population level, including most importantly those who never visit museums and archaeological sites. (2017a, 12–13)

Moshenska makes a sound point about the pressing issue of methodological integrity in public engagement. But, until those large-scale studies and systematic meta-analyses about the public are readily available, curators should aim for better-informed decisions about the public using available resources. Good practices already in place can facilitate the leap from being guided by arbitrary assumptions to making evidence-based decisions to a great extent. Adopting an evaluation strategy, consulting visitor research literature and collaborating with audience specialists are practices that ensure methodological standards are met in exhibition development.

Systematic evaluation and collaboration with audience specialists were – at the time – two novel features of the Money Gallery exhibition development. Front-end evaluation revealed some of the visiting public's attitudes towards money and its history, while formative evaluation assessed the suitability of certain gallery features for target audiences (Nomikou 2012). The evaluation results offered more confidence to the curators about the direction of their plans. Such confidence was needed because the decision to go for a more eased than a traditional disciplinary approach could potentially cause a risk to their professional credibility if not successful. It is essential to add at this point that the curatorial team, who were not accustomed to audience-related practices as part of their curatorial remit, begun to accept them only when they were reassured about the methodological soundness of those practices. Being subject specialist themselves, they could see how the system and tools of a different field – that of audience research – offered a reliable approach. The disciplinary credibility determined curatorial disposition towards a comprehensive audience consultation process.

Both evaluation and the collaboration with audience specialists helped curators develop a more public-oriented frame of mind with regards to the new gallery and more generally. My ethnographic data analysis suggests this shift by documenting increasing, and more insightful conversations between curators about prospective visitors as the exhibition process developed. My data also documents a shift in curatorial discourse and practice regarding the audiences for these collections over-all. From an abstract construct of non-specialist visitors and imagined critics, the prospective audience of the new gallery became a palpable entity with a range of identities, different types of knowledge and certain dispositions. As the public was rendered tangible and real, curators grew more sensitive towards sensing its needs. They started to utilise opportunities for audience consultation outside the scheduled evaluation sessions on a more informal basis. For example, the outreach sessions for primary schools did not only serve as a setting to test the gallery texts aimed at Key Stage 2 (aged 7–11) pupils but also as an opportunity to listen to what pupils were saying during coin handling. These and other comments, made by members of the public during coin handling sessions, became talking points concerning the gallery plans between curators. I do not wish to suggest that these instances were in any way systematic that could count as evidence-based material. Rather, they are indicative of the shift in practice with curators paying attention to what potential audiences had to say. These opportunities for curators to connect with real visitors and non-visitors 'out there' sustained a public-oriented frame of mind throughout the exhibition development process.

Implementation

The leap from arbitrary assumptions to evidence-based insights about the public is as crucial as is the next stage, *i.e.* the utilisation of said evidence. For all their methodological rigour, evaluation and visitor research have little or no impact unless their results and recommendations are implemented. Even if these practices are embedded in exhibition development, curators should be willing to adopt their findings and prepared to change plans as a result.

In the case of the Money Gallery, evaluation findings and recommendations from audience specialists were indeed utilised by the curatorial team with good results. Among other things, two features of the gallery best exemplify the implementation of specific audience consultation suggestions. First, it was the recognition that people, the prospective visitors, do not only engage with coins on an intellectual level but may well respond emotionally to the subject of money. Curators became more sympathetic to this revelation and, as a result, the tone of the gallery was modified to reflect it. There were instances where humour was employed to address people's complicated relationship with money. This had certainly not been the case when the numismatics department approached exhibitions before.

Another result of implementing audience research findings was the decision to place displays aimed at children in a central position along the long axis of the new gallery. Rather than being tucked away in the corner of the gallery to be used as an add-on resource by schools, the children-friendly cases became focal points in the gallery space, adding to its more relaxed feel. This bold move, illustrated with large cartoon imagery and surrounded by several interactive components, showed that curators were prepared to reach out of their comfort zone of traditional numismatic displays to involve audiences not traditionally engaged with these collections. The critical point in the transition was that curators started to pay closer, analytic attention to those audiences there were trying to reach. In exhibition development terms, the volume of curatorial time and labour spent on the children-oriented displays was similar to that spent on gallery components such as chronological displays, hoards and the star objects of the gallery.

My ethnographic analysis documented the transition of curatorial practice from holding arbitrary assumptions about visitors to fully implementing evidence-based recommendations and findings of audience consultation. The public was rendered visible in the process and turned into a concrete, legitimate partner in exhibition practice. This transition was accompanied by growing confidence among curators in their adaptation as professionals to a more public-facing role. There was a fresh sense of openness among the curatorial team at the time, which was going to redefine their relationship with the public. This was evident both in curatorial discourse and actions and marked the departure from old practices that kept the public at a perceived safe distance.

Some Final Thoughts

With the hindsight of more than a decade of developments in public engagement since the study was conducted, one could argue that the performance of that particular curatorial team is about average in terms of current public engagement standards. In fact, the curators themselves at the time admitted that they could have done more. The sense of openness towards the public was enacted up to the point that they felt comfortable. In their own words, being 'too open could open a can of worms' with issues like repatriation of artefacts, representation and identity politics. This remark is not meant to downplay their achievement, but to serve as a reminder that public engagement is far from a box-ticking exercise to be completed and left. It is an ever-growing curatorial responsibility to the public. Revisiting this study and reflecting on what, at the time, was a substantial innovative approach to public engagement in numismatic exhibition practice, highlights how far the public engagement agenda has moved since. And it is the responsibility of curators to engage with this agenda in their practice.

The aim of this chapter was to highlight the importance of rendering the public visible to curatorial exhibition practice. It suggests that three basic steps involved in the process: the *vocalisation* of curatorial assumptions about prospective audiences, the *consultation of evidence-based data* about the public, and the *implementation* of recommendations and findings in exhibition design. These steps can help curatorial teams make better-informed decisions about their exhibitions regarding the public. At the same time – and perhaps most importantly – they contribute to establishing a curatorial mindset that is geared towards the public. To develop this frame of mind is a decision that can be taken on individual and departmental/organisation-wide levels. As the next generation of curators in museums with collections of the ancient world takes over, this could be a rewarding challenge to take on.

References

Center for the Advancement of Informal Science Education (CAISE), https://www.informal-science.org

Dawson, E. (2018) Reimagining Publics and (Non) Participation: Exploring Exclusion from Science Communication Through the Experiences of Low-income, Minority Ethnic Groups. *Public Understanding of Science* 27 (7), 772–86.

Feinstein, N. & Meshoulam, D. (2014) Science for What Public? Addressing Equity in American Science Museums and Science Centers. *Journal of Research in Science Teaching* 51 (3), 368–94.

Hauptman Wahlgren, K. & Svanberg, F. (2008) Public Archaeology as Renewer of the Historical Museum. *Public Archaeology* 7 (4), 241–58.

Labrador, A. & Silberman, N. A. (eds) (2018) *The Oxford Handbook of Public Heritage Theory and Practice.* London, Routledge.

Litt, E. (2012) *Knock, Knock. Who's There? The Imagined Audience. Journal of Broadcasting & Electronic Media* 56 (3), 330–45.

Macdonald, S. (2002) *Behind the Scenes at the Science Museum.* London, Berg

Merriman, N. (ed.) (2004*) Public Archaeology.* New York, London, Routledge.

Moshenska, G. (2017a) Introduction: Public Archaeology as Practice and Scholarship Where Archaeology Meets the World. In G. Moshenska (ed.), *Key Concepts in Public Archaeology,* 1–13. London, UCL Press.

Moshenska, G. (ed.) (2017b) *Key Concepts in Public Archaeology.* London, UCL Press.

Moussouri, T. (2014). From 'Telling' to 'Consulting': A Perspective on Museums and Modes of Public Engagement. In S. Thomas & J. Lea (eds), *Public Participation in Archaeology,* 11–22. Woodbridge, Boydell and Brewer.

Nomikou, E. (2012). The Other Side of the Coin: Audience Consultation and the Interpretation of Numismatic Collections. In J. Fritsch (ed.), *Museum Gallery Interpretation and Material Culture,* 165–76. London, Routledge.

Nomikou, E. (2013) *A Museological Approach to Numismatic Exhibitions. An Exhibition Making Ethnography in the Ashmolean Museum.* Unpublished PhD thesis, University College London

Thomas, S. & Lea, J. (eds) (2014) *Public Participation in Archaeology.* Woodbridge, Boydell and Brewer.

Whitehead, C. (2009) *Museums and the Construction of Disciplines: Art and Archaeology in Nineteenth century Britain.* London, Duckworth.

Chapter 9

Steps Towards the Learning Museum: The National Archaeological Museum 'Inside Out'

*Maria Lagogianni-Georgakarakos, Despina Kalessopoulou,
Panagiota Koutsiana and Maria Selekou*

Introduction

The National Archaeological Museum, founded in Athens in 1866 to host antiquities
from all over Greece, is the oldest museum in the country, heir to the first National
Museum founded in 1829 at the provisional capital of the New Greek state, Aegina.
Its statutory purpose was to promote 'the study and teaching of the archaeological
science, the diffusion of archaeological knowledge and the development of love for
the fine arts' (Royal Decree of 31.7.1893). It is housed in a neoclassical building, a
monument itself, home to a vast range of collections from the 6th millennium BC to
the 5th century AD. The exhibition spaces cover 8000 m², where approximately 11,000
objects are exhibited from the Prehistoric, Sculpture, Vases, Minor Arts and Metalworks
Collections. Finally, the unique (for Greece) Collection of Egyptian Antiquities is displayed with works of art, dating from the predynastic period (5000 BC) to the time of
the Roman conquest. Behind the scene, 200,000 objects are kept in the storehouses
and five conservation workshops provide for the conservation and restoration needs
of the NAM's collections, as well as assisting in the conservation and collection care
of other state museums around the country. The National Archaeological Museum
receives annually around 600,000 visitors. It is the most frequented museum in Athens
after the Acropolis Museum.

Education has been perceived to be one of its core functions since the museum's
establishment. In its statutory purpose, a didactic approach to the collections was
strongly emphasised. For a museum founded in the 19th century this comes of no
surprise as the transmission of objective knowledge, diligently structured with
the help of various taxonomic systems, is the prevailing learning strategy

(Peponis & Hedin 1982; Hein 1998, 16–21). Although didacticism is still the predominant form in exhibitions today, as it is convenient and comfortable for both curators and traditional museum visitors (Black 2005, 130–1), visitor research along with new but well-established learning theories and societal changes have questioned the ways museums can fulfil their educational potential and increase public engagement. And here is where the notion of the 'Learning Museum' has come into play.

The Learning Museum relates to the concepts of the 'Learning Society' and the 'Learning Organisation', which can be defined as 'an organisation that is continually expanding its capacity to create its future' (Senge 1990, 14). We live in a world of constant change and, since our societies are in a continuous process of transformation with no stable state, we must become adept at learning to be able to manage these changes (Schön 1973). Lifelong learning has entered the agenda of the developed countries, going beyond educational systems (Faure *et al.* 1972, xxxiii) to include all agencies and activities that permit the sharing of knowledge and information (Husen 1974) for the sake of empowerment, self-development and self-realisation. Learning organisations, a term appearing in the management literature at the early 1990s, identify, promote and evaluate the quality of learning processes (Tsang 1997; Easterby-Smith & Araujo 1999, 2), to change into institutions that are learning systems, capable of bringing about their own continuing transformation (Schön 1973, 28).

Museums were traditionally seen as learning places, where people come to find expert knowledge and resources that connect with our collective memory. Yet, contemporary museums, living in a world of competitive leisure opportunities and a vast range of free-choice learning (Falk & Dierking 2000, 205–32) available readily due to new technologies, need to go beyond the linear model of providing knowledge and be responsive to their communities to engage them in a recurrent, profound and fulfilling way. A strategy to attain this is to invest in the internal culture of the museum, building on social capital, and become a learning organisation: an organisation that enters into dialogue with the internal and external audience to advance understanding and human well-being and to build shared values and vision; that fosters inquiry, making it safe for people to share openly and take risks; that embraces creative tension as a source of energy and renewal; that provides continuous learning opportunities for all and uses learning to reach its goals; that is continuously aware of and interacts with the surrounding environment (Kerka 1995).

However, critique has been expressed for the shortcomings of applying this model and the difficulty to find real-life examples of learning organisations (Smith 2001/2007). As Penny West suggests, the learning organisation, or the learning museum in our case, should be best thought of as a journey, not a destination (West 1994), where you may never arrive. It is a philosophy, not a programme, a vision that sees the world as interdependent and changing (Kerka 1995, 4).

It is the steps of this journey that we aim to discuss in this paper. We will focus on the education services of the National Archaeological Museum as the main taskforce for attaining change and enhancing public value. However, one should always bear in mind that the learning museum is not confined in the education department, but involves all aspects of the museum, be it collections, visitor services, research, conservation, *etc*. The museum should work as a learning network, both inwards and outwards. Employing this network, it can transform into a hub that makes archaeology public, thus relevant and more meaningful to its visitors.

Setting the Ground: Learning to Connect

The National Archaeological Museum has always been one of the leading destinations for school visits from all over Greece and abroad. Schoolbooks, art and history books are primarily illustrated with our collection objects, and people from all around the world consider the museum a must-see venue for Ancient Greek art. Bearing in mind that educational programmes in Greek museums have started developing from the 1980s onwards (Chrissoulaki & Pini 2008), the National Archaeological Museum has been a pioneer as it was the first archaeological museum that designed and implemented an educational programme for primary and secondary students, which ran throughout the school year 1979–80 in the context of the temporary exhibition *The Child in Antiquity* (Kalessopoulou 2017, 230). However, it was not until 2005 that the museum established a distinct Department of Public Relations and Education, shortly after a legislative change in the organisational structure of the Greek public archaeological museums and managed to systematise its educational provision by recruiting specialised staff. We soon standardised a range of educational programmes covering all levels of primary and secondary education. We embarked on discovering our visitors' specific aspirations and interests by inviting and collaborating with diverse groups of the community.

The educational objectives, common for all types of programmes that were set right from the beginning were:

- To help visitors get acquainted with ancient Greek culture
- To familiarise them with the museum as a place for learning and entertainment
- To promote active participation and creative expression
- To stimulate curiosity and develop critical thinking
- To cultivate fantasy and involve all senses and emotion
- To connect ancient culture with everyday experiences
- To promote collaboration and a sense of collectivity and belonging.

Under these new priorities, it is worth mentioning the strategic criteria by which the educational offer of the National Archaeological Museum was designed. Our primary goal was to promote greater engagement with our collections and to enable people to connect with the museum in ways that are meaningful to them. However, repositioning the museum was our major strategic investment. Although the museum is well known, visitor numbers by Greek citizens are rather low, often remaining a distant experience they had during school years. Therefore, we design educational services that are mostly based on face-to-face interaction for two reasons: a) inter-personal communication is the most preferred way by people in all societies to learn and associate with a subject or place (Bruner 2002); and b) we wanted our visitors to connect the National Archaeological Museum with a human face, friendly, recognis-able and familiar. We aspired for visitors to think of the museum as a place where people are waiting to welcome them and discuss, share knowledge and feelings with them, people that act as mediators for transforming the museum and its collections to a lively forum and a stage for sharing human experience.

Starting from schools, we knew that independent school visits are usually based on a pattern of an hourly tour at the highlights of the museum, provided by their teachers or by professional guides. We opted to structure our educational programmes differently, to promote a deep and joyful approach of various topics related to diverse aspects of Ancient Greek culture. Sharing Merriman's vision of a model of multiple perspectives in Public Archaeology, according to which the primary aim of people's involvement with archaeology is the encouragement of self-fulfilment, self-reflection, creativity and the enrichment of their lives (Merriman 2004, 7), we designed educa-tional programmes that are primarily based on inquiry-based learning and prompt for self-expression.

Year after year we further developed our pedagogical strategies by incorporating a wide range of pedagogical methods. Our knowledge of new and innovative techniques was enhanced through reading or seminars, experimentation, peer-to-peer learning. We also took advantage of our different talents in storytelling, puppet theatre, arts and crafts, music or dance, to enrich our offerings. Soon we realised both from our expanding experience as well as from informal comments and formal evaluation with students and educators, that schoolchildren, especially high-school children, were yearning for a different approach that had nothing to do with worksheets resem-bling schoolwork. They needed opportunities to express themselves and explore their identity by trying out different roles and by stepping into the shoes of people that lived a long time ago, leaving material traces of their adventures, beliefs and life habits in our collections. Theatrical improvisations became a trusted element of our educational programmes (Fig. 9.1), while experiments with creative writing showed great potential both for children and adults.

Educators and school representatives are considered equal collaborators to museum staff so, often, meetings with them are arranged to share knowledge of the collections as well as expertise from working daily with children. In this way, museum staff and educators learn how to learn together and create the best experiences for children. Sometimes we embark on joint long-term projects; occasionally, we host the work done in schools inspired by the museum (Fig. 9.2). For example, in the context of the International Museum Day in 2014, which was dedicated to the theme 'Museum collections make connections', we collaborated with the 1st Experimental Junior High School of Athens on a month-long programme. Students had the opportunity to be acquainted with the jewellery collections of the museum over a series of visits and

Figure 9.1: Theatrical improvisation of High School students during an educational programme (image: © National Archaeological Museum, Athens).

discussions with the education personnel. They then created their own jewellery from bronze, inspired by the museum collections. Their creations were exhibited for a week in a special area of the museum galleries and children participated in the way jewellery could be displayed, creating their interpretive panels.

Considering engagement with collections, new technologies are always a hot issue as to how well they can be integrated with the collection and whether they end up being 'in competition' with the real collections. The National Archaeological Museum promotes direct contact with the collections; however, technology is also used in a way that helps children and adult visitors engage and enquire more about the collection during their visit or at home. For example, an internet educational application aimed at teenagers for one of the NAM's most famous exhibits, the Antikythera Mechanism, encouraged children to participate in revealing the mysteries associated with its construction, function and use, by adopting a different vocational profile to conduct their online research (e.g. archaeologist, epigrapher, engineer and science historian).

Figure 9.2: Junior High Schools students create their own jewels inspired by the museum collections (image: © National Archaeological Museum, Athens).

The application was created as one of the educational services that would accompany the temporary exhibition of the Antikythera shipwreck (2012–2014). Yet, it remained available after the end of the exhibition, inviting children to discover the Mechanism and the other finds of the shipwreck through the internet and be more prepared on what to look for when they would be able to visit the museum. Supplementary information on the ongoing research for the Mechanism and the archaeological expedition at Antikythera was also made available via the Museum's website.

According to worldwide surveys, visitation of children in family groupings can account for 30% of total museum visitors (Falk 1998). Children are also very influential on the family's decision to visit a museum, while children's museum memories will have an impact on their attitudes as adults towards the museum (McManus 1989; Hooper-Greenhill 1994; MORI 2001; Wu 2008). To encourage family visitation, the National Archaeological Museum created in 2006 its first family programme named *The Fairytale of Sunday* that ran once or twice per month with the participation of professional storytellers and musicians. The regularity of the programme, as well as the fact that it was structured around a performance (the narration of myths and relevant folk fairytales with the accompaniment of live music inside the exhibition halls), rendered the activity compatible with other types of family outings in Athens (*i.e.* theatrical or music performances) and developed a steady audience. The programme remediated the rather fragmentary way Greek mythology is taught at schools and helped families connect the oral tradition of ancient Greeks with the material remnants of this unique culture. A short presentation of relevant archaeological artefacts at the end of the event that families could then look for in the museum galleries, offered the incentive to explore the museum in a self-led but focused and fun way.

Activity-based exploration and personal associations with the collections are also encouraged by the educational material available free for families at the museum's reception. Family events are regularly organised during school vacations, temporary exhibitions or special occasions, such as the International Museum Day, the European Heritage Days, *etc.* All these programmes and events allow families to approach our collections in alternative ways. Their seasonal cycle builds an audience that anticipates the events when the occasion arrives. Usually, these special occasions or celebrations are designed or coordinated by the Directorate of Museums at the Ministry of Culture, something that greatly supports the dissemination of the event's details and public awareness of their role and existence.

Nevertheless, children and grown-ups are eager to participate in any event or occasion that enables them to spend quality time with their family, learn something worthwhile and have the opportunity to pursue personal interests and gain new experiences (Hood 1983, 51). During the first years of programmes that were offered on weekends and holidays, we had a steady demand by parents and carers to participate together with their children or observe the education procedure, rather than stroll around freely while waiting to pick up their children after the end of the event. We gradually embarked in designing family programmes with joint participation, as well as programmes that families and also adults that were not accompanying children could participate alongside, such as the sketch sessions led by artists. In the more recent years our biggest success in terms of Public Archaeology activities and joint participation of children and adults was the *Find the city in the Museum* event, a treasure game that required the public to visit 12 different locations in the city centre, original findspots of sculptures now exhibited at the National Archaeological Museum, and collect stickers when successful. Those that managed to collect all stickers in their leaflet were welcomed free of charge at the National Archaeological Museum for an archaeologist-led guided tour to the exhibits, while the first 60 gained museum publications. Around 1500 visitors arrived at the museum with their completed leaflets during the four hours that the event took place. What is worth mentioning additionally is that this activity was collaboratively designed and implemented not only by the museum staff but also from a very active volunteer group in Athens called 'Atenistas-Athenians in Action', that designs events promoting awareness and active participation of all citizens, in order to improve cultural, environmental and social aspects of the city. The event formed part of a multifarious programme of actions that the National Archaeological Museum developed during 2016 for the celebration of the 150 years' anniversary since the foundation of its emblematic building.

The events described above also denote a 'paradigm shift' in the Museum's perception and practice while creating learning opportunities for the public. Specialised education personnel are essential; however curators, conservators, painters, sculptors, front of house staff, literally every employee of the museum, can interact and engage with the public in order to learn how to make their work more accessible and comprehensible, and to give people the opportunity to gain insights behind the scenes. *The Unseen Museum*, a curator-led initiative that involves exhibiting a different object from the Museum's stores in a central gallery every two months, accompanied by an enhanced narrative and discussion developed by curators, was enthusiastically welcomed by the press and public alike. This new format of events, was the first systematic educational activity with interpersonal interaction, delivered entirely by curatorial staff. The Conservation Department followed this example in the next year with a series of public engagement activities called *The Open Museum* incorporating expert-led lectures, demonstration of conservation procedures and tours of the conservation labs.

Steps like these help the learning museum proceed effectively towards its goals and connect museum audiences with the material culture of the ancient world, as well as the museum as an institution with the wider community in more profound and fulfilling ways.

Stepping Out, Bringing In

We will now turn to a set of outreach programmes targeted at special audiences: groups of people that confront physical or mental barriers that prevent them from visiting the museum and the actions taken by the National Archaeological Museum in order to help them overcome those. The Museum always strives to respond to requests from various groups of the community. We offer tailor-made programmes or adapt existing ones in order to serve the needs and aspirations of marginalised groups: people with learning or sensory disabilities, people with mental disorders, young people in drug rehabilitation programs, inmates in prisons and patients in hospitals. Common ground for all these programmes are the aims of facilitating physical access and independence while moving around and exploring the collections, as well as of creating meaningful experiences by enabling intellectual access to the collections.

Here, we present in detail the example of actions taken to support blind and partially sighted people, one of the earliest programmes we developed for people with disabilities. The Museum first produced a catalogue of 17 sculptures that may be touched, which has been available upon request at the Museum's reception since 2004, however in 2006 an invitation from the international organisation *Art beyond*

Sight to participate in the worldwide homonymous campaign, running each October, offered us the incentive to establish a systematic programme, specially tailored for this group. Each year we choose a different topic, *i.e.* the art of clay or music in antiquity, or the Antikythera shipwreck, that can be explored by touch and discussion (Fig. 9.3). The visit is structured in two parts: we begin with a haptic workshop where participants can touch replicas as well as authentic artefacts and discuss details of the selected topic with the museum educators. Afterwards, we tour the relevant exhibition galleries, offering a rich in mental imagery description, accompanied by touch where possible, and providing ground for a conversation that connects with issues common across the ages, such as play, marriage etc. Programmes addressed to children always end with an art workshop. The service is available all year round for interested visitors, although people expect and usually ask for it in October; we also have established a good collaboration with associations for blind and partially sighted people, that help us not only learn the particularities of the group but forward communication to its members.

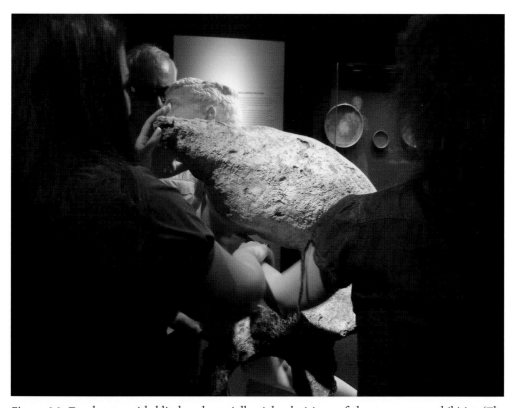

Figure 9.3: Touch tour with blind and partially sighted visitors of the temporary exhibition 'The Antikythera shipwreck' (image: © National Archaeological Museum, Athens).

The Museum has been further active in creating programmes for those who are unable to come to the museum, thus programmes where the Museum travels to their premises. An excellent case study is the NAM's collaboration with the education authority (prison school) of the female prison of Eleonas, Thebes, situated two hours away from Athens. When the prison's education authority requested the Museum's collaboration to enhance the school's curriculum, the Museum responded immediately. Several educational topics were chosen that had relevance to some of the life experiences of the prison's inmates, and for which the Museum possessed a wealth of material culture to illustrate from, including replicas that could be brought to the prison premises and be touched. Some of the topics explored included marriage, or the position of women in society. The same criteria were applied during the creation of an outreach programme for a second prison, this time for young offenders in Athens. In this case, the topic selected was ancient toys, as play is a universal experience. As one of the challenges while delivering these sessions was that some young offenders had limited understanding of modern Greek, holding a replica *e.g.* of an ancient toy, gave them the opportunity to participate without needing to describe the object, by simply experimenting and showing to others how they could use it. The group of young offenders being multicultural also meant that they were able to ascribe different meanings and uses to the ancient toys presented during the sessions, according to their own cultural experiences. All sessions at prison schools were accompanied by an artistic workshop, which offered an alternative way to connect the material culture presented with the inner thoughts and feeling of the participants.

We cannot stress enough the importance of collaborating closely with the expert staff of these institutions. They help the Museum staff to familiarise with the daily routine of their organisations and with the mental, psychological and physical state of the participants, offering a safety net during the first public engagement attempts, and a valuable evaluation for improving next steps. Results of these evaluations became apparent when the NAM started a new collaboration with one of the major children's hospitals in Greece, which was preceded by a set of meetings with teachers, social workers and psychologists before visiting the hospital wards to deliver the programme.

Outreach programmes of this kind extend their objectives beyond factual knowledge to aims of personal and social development. They contribute to a sense of normality and well-being as they create a valuable connection with reality outside the hospital or the prison and enhance the participants' social contacts through interactions with the museum staff (Kalessopoulou 2002).

Conclusion: Learning to Engage, Learning to Sustain

The National Archaeological Museum has opened up and tested new ways to approach traditional and non-traditional museum audiences, enrich public understanding of archaeology and sustain interest and involvement in the Museum, by not only addressing people as visitors but also as collaborators. What we learned from this process with regards to public engagement could be summarised in the following points:

- Consistency in the pedagogical principles applied: visitors know that participation in our educational activities is associated with active engagement, constructive dialogue, multidisciplinary approach, creative expression, storytelling, *etc.* They know what to expect, yet they are frequently surprised with innovative strategies that serve these principles.
- Fresh looks to engage with the collections: puppet or shadow theatre, drama, music, literature, dance, artistic creations, rich narrations, offer new ways to interpret material culture in a personal and highly attractive way.
- As for the themes selected, everything that has a connection with our lives today, with the world around us, with the physical environment is a possibility. Archaeological collections reveal a wealth of information about the lives of people in the ancient world, yet they also reveal that these people shared similar concerns or hopes with us. Therefore, almost all aspects of ancient material culture have the potential to be used in public engagement, highlighting what unites us with the ancient world, or revealing what could be done or thought differently.
- Collaborations with different community agencies are valuable in expanding museum audiences, improving museum practice and cultivating a sense of familiarity between museum practitioners and community representatives.
- A steady flow of activities and standard events on public holidays and other occasions that the audience is aware of and is looking forward to is a reliable means in sustaining audience interest.
- Joining forces: the museum can better fulfil its educational and social mission when learning objectives and public engagement become an objective for all staff, and not only of the Education Department. Sharing the big vision, learning from each other's expertise and experience, and feeling part of a great team that makes museum practice more meaningful to as many as possible, including ourselves, can transform the organisation into a well-functioning learning environment, open, receptive and nurturing to new ways of thinking.

In this way, Public Archaeology, a new approach to a long-established discipline that welcomes alternative and more personal interpretations of what the past may mean for people in the present, is best served, leading to collective aspirations that make museum collections not only accessible but truly significant.

References

Black, G. (2005) *The Engaging Museum. Developing Museums for Visitor Involvement.* London, Routledge.
Bruner, J. (2002) *Making Stories. Law, Literature, Life.* London, Harvard University Press.
Chrissoulaki, S. & Pini, E. (2008) Το κόκκινο νήμα: αρχαιολογικές εκπαιδευτικές εκθέσεις. In N. Νικονάνου & Κ. Κασβίκης (eds). Εκπαιδευτικά ταξίδια στον χρόνο. Εμπειρίες και ερμηνείες του παρελθόντος, 208–37. Athens, Patakis.

Easterby-Smith, M. & Araujo, L. (1999) Organisational Learning: Current Debates and Opportunities. In M. Easterby-Smith, J. Burgoyne & L. Araujo (eds), *Organizational Learning and the Learning Organization. Developments in Theory and Practice*, 1–22. London, Sage.

Falk, J. (1998) Visitors: Who Does, Who Doesn't and Why. *Museum News* 77 (2), 38–43.

Falk, J. & Dierking, L. (2000) *Learning from Museums: Visitor Experiences and the Making of Meaning.* Walnut Creek, CA, Lanham/New York, Oxford, Altamira Press.

Faure, E. *et al.* (1972) *Learning to Be [the Faure Report].* Paris, UNESCO.

Hein, G. (1998) *Learning in the Museum.* London, Routledge.

Hood, M. (1983) Staying Away: Why People Choose not to Visit Museums. *Museum News* 61 (4), 50–7.

Hooper-Greenhill, E. (1994) *Museums and their Visitors.* London, Routledge.

Husen, T. (1974) *The Learning Society.* London, Methuen.

Kalessopoulou, D. (2002) Children's Museums in Hospitals. In R. Sandell (ed.), *Museums, Society, Inequality*, 190–9. London, Routledge.

Kalessopoulou, D. (2017) National Archaeological Museum 1866–2016: From the Teaching of the Science of Archaeology to the Challenge of the Multifaceted Museum Experience. In M. Lagogianni-Georgakarakos (ed.), *Odysseys*, 211–36. Athens, Archaeological Receipts Fund.

Kerka, S. (1995) *The Learning organization: Myths and Realities.* Columbus, OH, ERIC Clearinghouse. http://files.eric.ed.gov/fulltext/ED388802.pdf (accessed 19 February 2015).

McManus, P. (1989) What People Say and How They Think in a Science Museum. In D. Uzzell (ed.), *Heritage Interpretation 2: The Visitor Experience*, 156–65. London, Belhaven Press.

Merriman, N. (2004) Introduction: Diversity and Dissonance in Public Archaeology. In N. Merriman (ed.), *Public Archaeology*, 1–17. London, Routledge.

MORI (2001) *Visitors to Museums and Galleries in the UK.* London, Council for Museums Archives and Libraries.

Peponis, J. & Hedin J. (1982) The Layout of Theories in the Natural History Museum. *9H* (3), 21–6.

Schön, D. A. (1973) *Beyond the Stable State. Public and Private Learning in a Changing Society.* Harmondsworth, Penguin.

Senge, P. (1990) *The Fifth Discipline: The Art & Practice of The Learning Organization.* New York, Currency Doubleday.

Smith, M. K. (2001/2007). The Learning Organization. *The Encyclopedia of Pedagogy and Informal Education*, http://www.infed.org/biblio/learning-organization.htm (accessed 19 February 2015).

Tsang, E. (1997) Organizational Learning and the Learning Organization: A Dichotomy Between Descriptive and Prescriptive Research. *Human Relations* 50 (1), 57–70.

West, P. (1994) The Learning Organization: Losing the Luggage in Transit? *Journal of European Industrial Training* 18 (11), 30–38.

Wu, K-L. (2008) *Inside a Family Day Out: Understanding Decisions to Visit Museums.* Unpublished Thesis, University of Surrey.

Chapter 10

Sensory Approaches to Material Culture: Theories and Reality of the Imagined Sensorially-engaged Museum

Anastasia Christophilopoulou

Engaging with the Past in the Era of Cultural Anaesthesia

Attention to sensory theories and methodologies has filtered the study of material culture and the work of classicists, archaeologists and historians for some time; it has been an important dimension of the dialogue between anthropology and material culture studies for much longer (Classen 1997; Edwards *et al.* 2006; Day 2013). However, the emerging field of 'Archaeology of the Senses' or 'Sensorial Archaeology' has proven very evasive and challenging for museum curators and museum professionals, many of whom originate from the Classical, art historical or archaeological discipline. During the past two decades we have observed more attempts to incorporate sensory theory and practice as part of archaeological field projects than we have seen it among museums. Museum curators, conservators and public engagement specialists are very used to examining, describing and of course, writing or talking about objects. Their practice has traditionally been empirical, although during the past 20 years it has been diversified by a plethora of analytical techniques and new technologies, allowing them to understand and experience objects in a different way. Still, either through traditional observation or by observation allowed by new technologies, museum curators and archaeologists, are not deprived of the ability to use their senses to experience and understand ancient material culture: vision, touch and smell are regularly used to approach the shape, function, materials, condition and deterioration of objects. Many museum curators and conservators are also experienced field archaeologists, meaning they are even closer to understanding the context of the archaeological objects they now care for, as well as the environment surrounding their sites of discovery. This all leads to an enhanced sense of material experience and temporality, surrounding not just the objects themselves, but also the world that created them.

Based on the above one would expect that, for professionals of this kind, material culture certainly manifests sensorial properties and requires sensory skills to approach it adequately. One might also expect that as museum curators can better understand the relationship between material culture and the sensory qualities of objects they curate or the sensory experiences implicated during their production, decoration, handling and use, they will be happy and willing to open up this experience to museum audiences. The truth is, they are. However, we do experience challenges and obstacles in either framing a methodological base under which we can start disseminating sensorial properties of our collections to the wider public or when we try to develop a practice to do this. In this chapter I explore how current theories and methodologies of sensory archaeology and sensory approach to material culture can and should relate to, and affect, museum theory and practice. I do this with an emphasis in Classical Collections, drawing examples from the Fitzwilliam's Greek, Roman and Cypriot collections, discussing recently implemented case studies with a conscious or 'incidental' sensorial approach. I also focus on what prevents us from establishing this practice on a wider scale and what needs to change to allow for sensorial experiences to be acknowledged as one of the learning and engagement aspirations of the modern museum.

The importance of the bodily senses into shaping human experience is undeniable, or to use Hamilakis's expression, a 'truism' (Hamilakis 2013a, 2). How we perceive and experience the material world that surrounds us is a result of how our senses respond to it. Moreover, these lived experiences then become part of our corporeal memory and cognition and help us establish new experiences and ultimately learned behaviours when faced with similar or new stimuli (Connerton 1989). For example, the smell of food usually stored in a particular type of container will evoke the desire to taste it, and when this container is being used repeatedly to store this particular foodstuff, seeing it on its own, without containing any food may evoke the memory of the food usually stored in it. In this example, two senses, smell and vision were involved in the production of experience, as well as to its transition to corporeal memory. In this case, the senses as the bearers and record-keepers of involuntary and pervasive material experience, also become potential sources of memory and temporality (Seremetakis 1994, 20).

While this is a straightforward example and, indeed, one that can be replaced by any of our everyday experiences with the material world, things become a little more complicated when it comes to experiencing material culture from the ancient world. The average museum visitor, when entering a gallery displaying antiquities from the ancient Mediterranean, is mostly faced with objects behind glass cases, some on open displays, but with restrictions as to how close one can get to them. The visitor is also faced with an exceptionally 'elite' category of ancient material culture, that is usually highly decorated, prestige objects, sculpture, or objects arising from 'privileged' taphonomic processes, such as closed archaeological contexts. For example, when visiting a gallery dedicated to the ancient Mediterranean, one is more likely to encounter decorated 5th-century BC pottery from a burial context than a set of everyday household pots of the same era. The reasons behind what material culture is more likely to end up on display in such a gallery are equally the results of complex archaeological procedures and taphonomic processes, as of centuries of collecting, giving and acquiring antiquities (Bourdieu & Alain 1990; Bennett 1995; Barringer & Flynn 1998). These reasons have been studied sufficiently elsewhere and are not the subject of this chapter; they are however of relevance: if we were to think of a suitable category of objects to initiate a sensory approach to our collections for our audiences, then it would be the utilitarian, everyday pottery and objects we would turn to first, rather than the unique sculptural pieces surviving, or the highly decorated 5th-century BC pots. This is because it would be easier to approach the sensorial aspects of an everyday object (*e.g.* whether its surface is polished and smooth, or rough because it is handmade and coarse) for the visitor first before we even have the chance to introduce him/her to what these might have meant for the ancient user who made/used this pot. Introducing ancient objects that have relevance to what modern people use today in their everyday lives is much more uncomplicated to introducing them to a sculptural piece or an object that cannot evoke any material culture experience and sensorial memory to their own life. The argument here principally agrees with two arguments expressed by David Lowenthal in his seminal work *The Past is a Foreign Country* (Lowenthal 1999): 'Surroundings, including surrounding material culture help make human beings aware of the past; also, human beings can salvage, reshape, and reorganize the past, through relics, monuments, architectural "preservations," reconstructions and exhibits'.

So far, we have seen what challenges may arise when museum professionals try to implement sensory practices in their public engagement efforts. In this, we admitted that traditional museum procedures, practices and even perceptions of conserving, maintaining and exhibiting artefacts might be clashing with sensorial approaches to material culture. However, the problem does not just arise from within the museum. Challenges, including what may prevent the public from seeking to engage with ancient world collections in a sensory way, may be related to modern life and the way we experience material culture today as a whole. Cultural anthropologists, sociologists and archaeologists to some extent (Seremetakis 1994, 19; Feldman 1994, 89; Hamilakis 2013a, 6) have argued that large numbers of people living today in the developed world are experiencing a strong disconnect with material culture. Hamilakis describes this as a 'state where the material world, other people, place, time, and history are experienced in a highly regulated bodily manner; where the affective import of sensorial experience is tightly controlled' (Hamilakis 2013a, 2). Feldman goes as far as describing living under these conditions as a state of 'cultural anaesthesia'. While this term might indeed be an overstatement and certainly cannot apply to everyone living in the western world, we cannot deny that some people are experiencing this condition. If we take into account that this phenomenon was described in the mid-1990s, paired with the dramatic acceleration of digital technology and the influence it had on our lives during the past two decades, it is safe to admit that a large proportion of people living in the developed world have limited opportunities to interact with material culture in a sensory-engaging way. The figure might be even more alarming in the case of young people and children. This creates a whole new level of challenge; if people are feeling disconnected to material culture, *e.g.* nature, materials and ways objects – they use and depend on every day – are made, they are certainly going to be less inclined to, or find it difficult to interact with ancient material culture in a sensory way.

Two Case Studies and a Paradox

I now want to turn to two distinct case studies from our practice in the Fitzwilliam Museum (one extending to programmes adopted across other University of Cambridge Museums). Both programmes have either incorporated sensory experience with the Fitzwilliam's collections or were built upon the sensory qualities/aspects of the objects used in them. It is important to note that both programmes were conceived, designed and implemented by a variety of museum professionals, in these cases, curators, educators and learning specialists, public engagement champions and people whose expertise is in engagement with disability groups.

The first programme began life as a specific action for blind and partially sighted people and took the form of touch tours in the collections of the Ancient Greece, Rome and Cyprus of the Fitzwilliam Museum. Initiated by the author, then a research associate for the Department of Antiquities charged with diversifying the range of outreach and public engagement activities of the newly refurbished Gallery of Ancient Greece and Rome, the programme implemented thematic touch tours across carefully selected groups of objects, large or small, in two consecutive galleries. As an idea, it was fully supported by the Keeper of Antiquities Dr Lucilla Burn, with whom the selection of objects was made, discussions on the creation of the accompanying content were held, and a generous amount of time was spent evaluating and refining the whole programme until it became established. Input from the department's specialist conservator, Ms Julie Dawson was also vital in selecting objects that were both safe and suitable for handling but also those that displayed the best features and characteristics for sensory engagement.

The programme run from the start with two distinct content units: a selection of sculptural items introducing our participants to the art and process of carving stone and marble into sculpture, and a group of 5th-century BC pottery from the domestic context (an amphora, a stemmed kylix, an oinochoe and a pyxis). For the pottery selection we also opted for the creation of two identical sets of replicas of the original objects, created on request by the Thetis Authentics laboratory for archaeological replicas, in Athens headed by Dr Eleni Aloupi, archaeologist and archaeometer. While one set was regularly used for the pottery thematic touch tours, the other was turned into an 'archaeological suitcase', which we regularly took to outreach sessions in Addenbrookes Hospital, Cambridge.

The sculptural group contained no more than five objects per tour. This might seem like a small selection but if one takes into account that we worked in small, almost one-to-one groups, where each participant was guided at the objects by a session leader, then five objects were more than enough to fill the best part of an hour. Two objects have been the highlight of this type of tour, a large Roman coffin (sarcophagus), the Pashley Sarcophagus (GR.1.1835), standing prominently at the centre of the refurbished Greek and Roman Gallery and purposely at a height equally accessible by the average standing visitor or a wheelchair user; and the marble torso of Dionysos from the Roman Gymnasium complex of Salamis in Cyprus (GR.2.1891), displayed in the A.G. Leventis Gallery of Ancient Cyprus, equally at a very accessible height.

The sarcophagus is made of marble and has a highly polished, carved front and an uncarved back (Fig. 10.1a). It is decorated with intricately carved figures showing Dionysos, the Greek god of wine, in procession with his followers the satyrs and maenads (Budde & Nicholls 1967, 161, pls 53–5; Vassilika 1998, 116–17). It is known in the Museum as the 'Pashley Sarcophagus', named after the man who first published it (in 1837), Robert Pashley. When the touch tour takes place in front of the sarcophagus, we aim to introduce our participants to the shape and dimensions of the object (including sharing information about its weight), but mostly the feel of the stone and the differences of the highly carved and polished side to the roughly carved back (Fig. 10.1b–d). When the participant has created a mental image of the object, we move to describe, by touch, every important episode of the intricate and 'crowded' procession, as if we were telling a story. We are telling the story of the coffin's iconography, figure by figure, detail after detail. We then wrap up by providing more information on the discovery of the object in the small harbour of Arvi in south Crete, its journey to Britain and into the museum's collections.

When working with the torso of Dionysos (GR.2.1891) in the Cyprus gallery, the tour takes a different format. The naked and partially surviving torso, with its garment flung over the left shoulder and draping over the forearm, dates to the 2nd century AD, but reflects a 4th-century BC 'Hermes Belvedere' type, also known earlier as 'Hermes Antinoos' type (Munro *et al.* 1891,131; Karageorghi *et al.*1999, 100–1; Christophilopoulou 2016, 13–19). This was a well-known Praxitelian type, used as a model for both Hellenistic and later Roman ruler portraits (Fig. 10.2) The emphasis when exploring this object by touch, is on the shape and posture of the body, the way its musculature and anatomic details are made 'visible' by the carving of the unknown but skilled sculptor. The experience, as described by one of our participants over the years, is: 'like touching a naked body; only that the flesh is replaced by the cold, smooth marble. It made me think of the great effort and ability the ancient sculptor must have possessed to create it'. It is a deeply sensorial experience for participants and session leaders alike. As with the case of the sarcophagus, we wrap up the session by mentally 'guiding' our participants to the rich archaeological heritage of Salamis on the East coast of Cyprus. This mental tour includes information on how the city enjoyed a long and prosperous history, starting in the 11th century

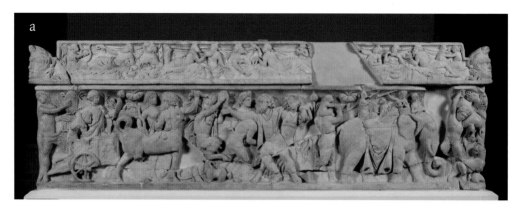

Figure 10.1: a: Marble sarcophagus (GR.1.1835) decorated with intricately carved figures showing Dionysos, the Greek god of wine, in procession with his followers the satyrs and maenads, from Arvi, south Crete, dated to the 2nd century BC (image: The Fitzwilliam Museum, 2013); b–d: blind and partially sighted tactile programmes (touch tours) in the Greek & Roman and Cypriot galleries of the Fitzwilliam Museum (image: Fitzwilliam Museum, 2020).

BC and ending with it becoming one of the major powers of the region during the Roman times.

The year 2020 marks the 9th year of the implementation of the touch tours as an engagement programme for the Department of Antiquities. Since 2011, we have hosted over 50 touch tours in Antiquities and fostered two strong partnerships with the Royal National Institute of Blind People (RNIB) and the local charity CamSight who supports people of all ages in Cambridgeshire living with low vision and blindness. What we are most proud of is that this small initial project gradually grew to a scaled-up programme now adopted across curatorial departments of the Fitzwilliam and led by several experts within our Learning and Public Engagement teams, but also across the University of Cambridge Museums consortium, with staff in each museum having received training to deliver touch tours (Clarke 2018; 2019). What we have gained by initiating this action is twofold: we developed a programme that actively built upon the sensory engagement with the ancient material world, and

Figure 10.2: Marble torso of Dionysos (GR.2.1891) from Salamis, Cyprus with its garment flung over the left shoulder and draping over the forearm, dated around the 2nd century BC. The type reflects a 4th-century BC 'Hermes Belvedere' prototype, also known earlier as 'Hermes Antinoos' (image: The Fitzwilliam Museum, 2020).

provided participants with the medium (touch) to experience an ancient object, but also to create a memory of the object and with it the memory of its historical and archaeological context. This sequence is very similar to what Cole had described as the creation of memory relying on the senses, and the senses relying on the materiality and the physicality of the world (Cole 1998).

Our second case study came ten years after the first, and it was a conscious decision by the Fitzwilliam Museum to explore the possibilities of sensory and sensorial engagement with the museum's collections, as well as investigate those arising by implementing virtual or augmented realities to original artworks. Sensual/Virtual (2019–2020) marked the first annual theme implemented at the Fitzwilliam, explored through temporary exhibitions, displays and events. As part of this season, we investigated the history of the production of archaeological replicas from the 19th century to today, fascinated by the biographies, manifold interpretations and uses of these replicas today and in the past. Other than interpretative questions about replicas, or questions surrounding the era of digital reproduction of material culture utilising 3D scanning, photogrammetry, 3D printed replicas and virtually recreated archaeological landscapes, and the contribution all these methods have to the debate between truth (original) and imitation (replica). We also addressed questions on the materiality of replicas, and the sensory experience received when handling or interacting with them, as well as joined other researchers (*e.g.* Eve 2018, 114–22) in questioning whether the production of 3D virtual replicas or artefacts is adequately supported by suitable information regarding the multi-sensory nature of artefacts.

We conducted this research as an experiment, leading to discussions and seminars, the production of extensive 3D scans and photogrammetry for a selection of objects from the Aegean and Cypriot collections of the Fitzwilliam and finally, the production of limited 3D printed replicas from the above group. We also prepared a special display containing rare late 19th-century gilt copper-alloy electrotype replicas of the original Vapheio (Laconia) cups decorated with reliefs featuring bulls, made by Émile Gilliéron (1850–1924), an archaeological illustrator for Heinrich Schliemann, alongside some newly 3D printed replicas.

Photogrammetry and 3D scanning were conducted by Daniel Pett, Head of Digital at the Fitzwilliam, supported by Dr Jennifer Wrexler, Creative Economy Engagement fellow for the Arts & Humanities Research Council-funded CEEF Project (Wrexler 2019; Pett 2019; Pett &Vine 2019). Together they produced a vast gallery of 3D imaging of our ancient Mediterranean collections which led to the in-depth study of certain categories of objects. Two 3D printed replicas of an ancient boat and statuette, resulting from this research, are indicative of the use of 3D technology to assist the study of museum objects and our explorations of the objects' sensory aspects. The first, a 3D-printed replica of a Cypriot limestone statuette, with inscription in Greek alphabet on its back, is based on an original from Amargetti, Cyprus (GR.239.1888), dating to the 3rd century BC. The statuette was dedicated to the pastoral god Opaon Melanthios, at a time when Cypriots had begun to embrace the pan-Mediterranean Greek alphabet in everyday life. The 3D printed replica is made from a gypsum material replicating the original limestone composition of the statue. When handled, one can understand how the ancient object was made, as well as feel the inscription on the back of the statuette. The second example is the 3D printed replica of a terracotta model of a warship. The original (Loan Ant.103.11) is a clay model of a Hellenistic warship, dated around the 3rd or 2nd century BC, with a flat base and thick uprights supporting a deck. The object was probably one of the most important warship models known from Cyprus. By creating this 3D printed replica of the boat, our audiences were able to handle it, gaining a better understanding of the tactile and sensory nature of an, otherwise, very fragile object.

The project's largest investment was the production of a large scale, high-quality replica of the statue of Dionysus (GR.2.1891) which is destined to be displayed permanently next to the original statue in the Cyprus gallery, offering a permanent tactile display for all (as opposed to the touch tours addressed to blind or partially sighted people on specific occasions). Thus, the large-scale replica would represent the first of the museum's actions to implement permanent tactile displays alongside original artworks (Fig. 10.3).

So, where does the paradox lie? So far, we have seen two case studies, originating from just one museum (with plenty more successful efforts coming from other European museums), displaying the clear message that introducing sensory content to the way we interpret our collections as museum professionals, and the way we offer them to interpretation to our audiences, is possible and should become standard practice. One side of the paradox lies in the fact the provision of a sensory experience was

Figure 10.3: 3D scans of the marble torso of Dionysus (GR.2.1891) from Salamis, used in the production of a high-quality replica for tactile display (images: Daniel Pett, 2020).

not always the main goal of the actions or projects we examined here. Some begun life as public engagement projects and the objects'/collections' sensory aspects became a medium enabling this engagement. In other words, enabling a sensory experience did not only enhance the interpretation of these objects but took a step into creating a more inclusive provision for the museum's audiences (Christophilopoulou 2019). The second side of the paradox, in that while we are quick to react and enable the opportunities brought by new technologies (3D scanning, digitally created replicas), we are still slow in debating what these methods bring in theoretically or methodologically in museum practice. In other words, we are working without a 'handbook' as to what these scientific advances bring to the field of humanities.

Uncasing the Senses: From 'Do not Touch' to the Era of Immersive Experiences

Museums and their theoretical counterpart, museology, as well as the discipline of Archaeology have experienced considerable advances during the past two decades, including opening to a sensory-driven theory and practice. However, in both disciplines, there is still a long way to go. In Archaeology, an otherwise 'intensely physical craft based on handling, closely observing, and drawing/photographing material things' (Hamilakis 2013b, 412) we sometimes fail to transmit the physicality of past objects by employing anything else but the sense of autonomous vision. This is important not just for communicating the discipline widely, but for us as practitioners in Archaeology: unless if we explore diverse sensorial and affective possibilities and their associated social meanings to our interpretations of the past, we will never get past the impasse of understating the material culture we excavate. In other words, we must experience why vessels have soft surfaces or rough surfaces, how they were decorated, fired and stored. It is equally important that we engage in thinking how these objects were experienced by different people, different genders and different social groups in the ancient world (Fig. 10.4). To achieve this, though, we must first recognise the need to train archaeologists adequately to respond to sensorial properties of material culture. This is by no means a straightforward path: many of us, archaeologists, curators or public engagement practitioners, find it difficult to navigate between the strict methodology and long-form narratives (Tringham 2015, 708) traditionally employed during our empirical or analytical observations of ancient objects, to incorporate sensorial awareness of the objects and ultimately also about the past.

Traditionally sight has been the only sense with a ticket to enter the museum. The same is true of histories of art, in which artworks are often presented as purely visual objects. In the *Museum of the Senses* Classen (2017) offers a new way of approaching the history of art through the senses, revealing how people used to handle, smell and even taste collection pieces. While considerable steps are being taken by the modern museum to engage with sensory approaches, we still lack a concrete interdisciplinary conversation with participation from the fields of Classics, Archaeology, History,

a

b

Figure 10.4: a: Red-polished tulip bowl and b: horn-lug handled bowl from Vounous, Cyprus, both dated to the Early Bronze Age (Early Cypriot I Period, c. 2400/2300–c. 2200 BC) When examining these objects, it is important to experience how the surface of the clay feels, how the objects stood or were suspended, as well as consider what they might have contained and who might have used them (images: Antiquities Department, Fitzwilliam Museum, 2020).

Philosophy and sensory theory. To these classic humanities fields, we must now add the fields of computer vision and augmented realities. The role of interactive and immersive technologies in transforming how we perceive and experience museum collections is undeniable. Still, discussions on how exactly to do this, and what we what to achieve across these disciplines, are only just starting. At the same time, we must admit that we cannot come up with a 'one-size fits all' museum model. As we accept that sensory perception is a cultural construct, we must also accept that individuals (museum practitioners or visitors) will attribute and engage with different sensory aspects based on their sensory models adopted socially.

Moving away from declarations of the 'vast museum of historical and sensory absence' (Feldman 1994, 104), statements which at the time they were made served the purpose of raising awareness for the things that out to change, this chapter ultimately argued that adopting sensorial approaches when engaging our museum audiences with our collections, is not just an advance in public engagement practice, but an essential way forward to a more inclusive museum approach.

References

Barringer, T. & Flynn, T. (eds) (1998) *Colonialism and the Object: Empire, Material Culture, and the Museum.* London, New York, Routledge.

Bennett, T. (1995) *The Birth of the Museum: History, Theory, Politics.* London, Routledge.

Bourdieu, P. & Alain, D. (1990) *The Love of Art: European Art Museums and their Public.* Stanford, CA, Stanford University Press.

Budde, L. & Nicholls, R. (1967) *Catalogue of the Greek and Roman sculpture in the Fitzwilliam Museum.* Cambridge, Cambridge University Press.

Christophilopoulou, A. (2016), Re-examining the History of Cypriot Antiquities in the Fitzwilliam Museum: A Look at the Collection's Past and Present. In G. Bourogiannis & C. Mühlenbock (eds), *Ancient Cyprus Today. Museum Collections and New Research*, 13–19. Uppsala, Astrom.

Christophilopoulou, A. (2019) *'Being an Islander' Project Overview.* Cambridge, Fitzwilliam Museum. https://www.fitzmuseum.cam.ac.uk/being-islander-art-and-identity-large-mediterranean-islands.

Clarke, R. (2018) *Sensing Culture: Insights into how to Improve the Visitor Experience for Blind & Partially Sighted People.* University of Cambridge Museums Blog. https://www.museums.cam.ac.uk/blog/2018/07/30/sensing-culture-insights-into-how-to-improve-the-visitor-experience-for-blind-partially-sighted-people/ (accessed 9 April 2020).

Clarke, R. (2019) *Curiosity & Creativity: Art Workshops for and with Blind and Partially Sighted Adults.* University of Cambridge Museums Blog. https://www.museums.cam.ac.uk/blog/2019/08/20/curiosity-creativity-art-workshops-for-and-with-blind-and-partially-sighted-adults/ (accessed 9 April 2020).

Classen, C. (1997) Foundations for an Anthropology of the Senses. *International Social Science Journal* 153, 401–12.

Classen, C. (2017) *The Museum of the Senses. Experiencing Art and Collections.* London, Bloomsbury.

Cole, J. (1998) The Work of Memory in Madagascar. *American Ethnologist* 25(4), 610–33.

Connerton, P (1989) *How Societies Remember.* Cambridge, Cambridge University Press.

Day, J. (2013) *Making Senses of the Past: Toward a Sensory Archaeology.* Carbondale, IL, Southern Illinois University Press.

Edwards, E., Gosden, C. & Philips, R. (eds) (2006) *Sensible Objects: Colonialism, Museums, And Material Culture.* Oxford, Berg.

Eve, S. (2018) Losing our Senses, an Exploration of 3D Object Scanning. *Open Archaeology* 4, 114–22.

Feldman, A. (1994) From Desert Storm to Rodney King via ex-Yugoslavia: On Cultural Anaesthesia. In N. Seremetakis (ed.), *The Senses Still: Perception and Memory as Material Culture in Modernity*, 87–107. Chicago, IL, University of Chicago Press.

Hamilakis, Y. (2013a) *Archaeologies and the Senses: Human Experience, Memory, and Affect.* Cambridge, Cambridge University Press.

Hamilakis, Y. (2013b) Afterword: Eleven Theses on the Archaeology of the Senses. In J. Day (ed.), *Making Senses of the Past: Toward a Sensory Archaeology.* Carbondale, IL, Southern Illinois University Press.

Karageorghis, V., Vassilika E. & Wilson P. (1999) *The Art of Ancient Cyprus in the Fitzwilliam Museum.* Cambridge, Cambridge University Press.

Lowenthal, D. (1999) *The Past is a Foreign Country.* Cambridge, Cambridge University Press.

Munro J., Tubbs & Wroth W. (1891) Excavations in Cyprus, 1890. Third Season's Work. Salamis, *Journal of Hellenic Studies* 12, 59–198.

Pett, D. (2019) *Photogrammetry work on the Greek and Roman Collections of the Fitzwilliam Museum, University of Cambridge.* https://museologi.st/photogrammetry/classical-busts-fitz

Pett, D. & Vine, J. (2019) *AHRC Creative Economy Engagement Fellowships.* https://creative-economy.fitzmuseum.cam.ac.uk/projects/project-four-miab-mediterranean/

Seremetakis, N. (1994) *The Senses Still: Perception and Memory as Material Culture in Modernity.* Chicago, IL, University of Chicago Press.

Tringham R. (2015) Review of Hamilakis Y., 'Archaeology and the Senses: Human Experience, Memory, and Affect, Cambridge University Press, 2013'. *European Journal of Archaeology* 18 (4), 705–48.

Vassilika, E. (1998) *Greek and Roman Art*. Cambridge, The Fitzwilliam Museum.

Wrexler J. (2019) *Creation of 3D printed replicas from the Fitzwilliam Museum's Ancient Mediterranean collection, as part of the Creative Economies project to be used as tactile displays, in collaboration with the 'Being an Islander' project.* https://creative-economy.fitzmuseum.cam.ac.uk/projects/project-four-miab-mediterranean/

Chapter 11

Casting Light on the Ancient World: Education in the Museum of Classical Archaeology, Cambridge

Jennie Thornber

Plaster cast collections offer a unique opportunity for teaching and public engagement with the ancient world, but when the objects are one step away from their ancient originals how can museum practitioners persuade visitors to take the collection seriously? This paper will focus on public engagement with the collection of plaster casts at the Museum of Classical Archaeology (MOCA), Cambridge. It will reflect on the advantages and challenges of teaching with a collection of casts from the point of view of a museum education practitioner. Case studies will be examined to illustrate successful ways Museum staff have found of engaging different strands of its audience with the collection through its public programming. First, I will explore how the collection offers plentiful opportunities to inspire children through family programming, citing examples which explore a variety of learning approaches. Then, I will consider how Museum staff have engaged with adults through Late events, alternative options for a night out which exploit MOCA's potential as a social space after-hours. These case studies showcase the broad range of activity MOCA offers to its audiences to provide meaningful learning experiences. First, I begin by giving a brief overview of the Museum and its collection.

The Museum of Classical Archaeology

MOCA is one of the world's finest collections of plaster casts of Greek and Roman sculpture. Its collection of over 450 casts covers a broad time period, beginning with casts of Archaic Greek sculpture from the 7th century BC and ending with Roman sculpture from the 5th century AD. Although MOCA is also home to a collection of ancient pottery, small artefacts, sherds and squeezes it is the casts which are its public face and by far its greatest asset when it comes to engaging audiences. In this section and the next, I provide an overview of the Museum's history, its collection, its purpose, and its audience. This is necessary background for appreciating the challenges of teaching with this collection and recognising the value of the educational approach taken in the two case studies which follow.

One of the University of Cambridge Museums, MOCA's educational role goes back to its foundation in 1884. In her article on the origins of the Museum, Beard (1994, 3) discusses the speeches made at the celebration of the founding of the Museum of Classical and General Archaeology, as it was then called, and observes that those championing this new institution identified two quite different functions for this new museum. First, they hoped that it would serve to educate the public in the beauty of Greek art, and perhaps inspire them in their own creativity. Secondly, they lauded the Museum as a place of learning for the emerging discipline of archaeology, with the Keeper of Greek and Roman Antiquities at the British Museum, Charles Newton, even going so far as to say that to teach archaeology without a cast museum was 'like trying to teach chemistry without a laboratory, or medicine without a hospital' (Beard 1994, 3). Nearly 130 years later, the Museum holds true to this educational philosophy: since the 1980s, it has shared a building with the Faculty of Classics and continues to play a part in undergraduate teaching.

The Museum of 1884, conceived as an archaeological laboratory for scholars and academics, insisted that 'children in arms and nursery maids with children are not admitted' (Beard 1994, 15). The Museum of 2020, however, is welcoming and inclusive to all, with its mission statement pledging to demonstrate 'to the widest possible audience the continuing importance and relevance of Classical Archaeology to the contemporary world' (Turner 2016, 2). It welcomes around 14,699

Figure 11.1: The Museum of Classical Archaeology as it looks today (image: Museum of Classical Archaeology, University of Cambridge).

members of the public each year, of which 6074 are children and young people on educational visits (data for 2018–19). As Hooper-Greenhill (2007, 13) notes, while an educational role was a key characteristic of 19th-century collections such as MOCA, it is no longer considered enough simply to display objects which visitors might learn from in order to fulfil this educational role. MOCA's education service now engages with diverse audiences, from primary and secondary school students, families and young adults, to people at risk of social isolation, such as those with cognitive or visual impairments, the homeless and vulnerably housed, and those suffering from poor mental health. Different approaches are adopted, reflecting the active role visitors take in their learning, to present opportunities for them to learn (Fig. 11.1).

A 'Museum of Lies': Audience Responses to a Museum of 'Fakes'

How do audiences respond to a collection of plaster casts? Rarely does it go unnoticed. Rarely is it not commented upon. Recognising this, Museum staff do not shy away from discussing the authenticity of the objects with its visitors: the topic is raised with every group visiting for a taught session. Often, they will be asked to guess the age of the sculptures as an opening gambit, and to consider whether they are disappointed to learn that the objects are not, in fact, over 2000 years old. As might be expected, the Museum's team finds that reactions vary.

In the case of some groups, most often secondary school students, Museum staff face the challenge of winning over sceptical participants. The Museum was once described by a young person visiting on a school trip as a 'museum of lies' – an epithet which serves as a gentle reminder to Museum staff to be as transparent as possible about the distinction between the casts and the original sculptures they replicate. On the other hand, primary school children invariably are not disappointed. For them, their first experience of the Museum when they step over the threshold is one of sheer awe: the larger-than-life sculptures which tower above them offer the perfect opportunity to immerse children in the ancient world. The chance to gaze upon the gods and mythological creatures they have read about in books or learnt about in the classroom brings these figures to life; for them, this appears to take precedence over authenticity. However, with some adult audiences, the status of the casts as replicas can pose a serious challenge to commonplace museum rules. It is not uncommon for visitors to touch the casts, assuming that it would not be forbidden to touch replicas. In contrast, other adult visitors would challenge the status of the casts as the purely educational tools they were originally collected to serve as some visitors see the casts as artworks in their own right, made by skilled craftsmen, or appreciate the casts as historical objects, with many having been crafted in the 19th century or earlier.

It is undeniable that one of the greatest advantages of the collection is its ability to teach the development of classical art – it has, of course, been formed with this express purpose in mind. This comprehensive collection, which comprises the superstars of the classical canon, enables MOCA to fulfil its original function in disseminating this knowledge not only to the University's Classics students but also to the general public. When Museum staff deliver sessions on classical art, visitors are invited to consider their disappointment at not being faced with original artefacts, but also the advantages of learning from the collection. With the original sculptures scattered across Europe and beyond, where else would they have the opportunity to see these particular sculptures side-by-side so that they might compare and contrast certain works? Students of Greek art and architecture (an optional module for A-level Classical Civilisation in the UK) are asked to discuss how the chance to study from casts compares with using their course textbooks back at school. Here, they can see intricate details up-close, they can view sculptures in the round and can get a sense of the scale of the sculptures. They can even debate the subject of polychromy, thanks to a pair of casts of the Peplos Kore: one vibrantly painted, the other showing the colour of white marble. Without a doubt, the gloomy black-and-white photographs in the students' textbooks struggle to compare.

So, are the casts just middle men? Indeed, the use of the casts within MOCA's learning service is often as a conduit for teaching about the ancient world more broadly, rather than purely as a basis for traditional art history. In this context, rather than focusing on the casts as a way to learn about the original sculptures, they are used to transport visitors back to the ancient world. The casts allow Museum staff to teach about the objects they replicate. Still, just as importantly, they also provide the perfect springboard for learning about a multitude of aspects of the ancient world: myth, religion, society and much more. For example, staff have used the casts to tell Greek myths to the youngest visitors and to teach about various aspects of life in the ancient world through creative and hands-on experiences during family events. Recently, the casts have also proven excellent prompts for discussing sexuality in the ancient world with adults not only through a museum trail, *Queer Antiquities* but also through volunteer-led LGBTQ+ tours given as part of the University of Cambridge Museums' Bridging Binaries programme.

What of the Casts as Casts – Historical Objects in their Own Right?

A range of recent events and exhibitions have confronted the status of the objects as replicas and celebrated them as objects in their own right. For example, the event *Casts by Candlelight* (2015), offered torch-lit tours which shared with visitors the stories behind how some of the casts came to be in the collection and explored the 18th- and the 19th-century context in which cast collections thrived. In 2018, artist Florian Roithmayr installed a series of sculptural interventions throughout the Cast Gallery as part of his research project *The Humility of Plaster* and explored the inheritances of cast-collecting and mould-making. Nevertheless, it is the casts' ancient – rather than modern – stories, which continue to hold the strongest appeal for visitors.

As a university museum embedded within an academic department, and mindful of the educational role it has inherited from its founders, MOCA proudly continues to use its collection to teach a range of audiences. However, its means of doing so have morphed radically since its foundation in line with the demands of its audiences, current research and methods in pedagogy and cultural programming. Although the Museum can face challenges in getting some strands of its audience to take the collection seriously, its strengths lie in its versatility: not only is it ideally suited for teaching Greek art but it is also an excellent springboard for branching out into a plethora of aspects of the ancient world. The Museum strives to be creative, exciting and innovative in all areas of public engagement but I would now like to focus on two case studies which examine approaches to public programming for two very different audiences – families and adults – which exemplify how the Museum uses these strengths to its advantage.

Family Programming

MOCA is proud to be a family-friendly space. The family programme is an integral part of its public engagement work. It offers events for families with children throughout the year, largely in the school holidays in order to serve its local community. Its events are always free of charge and usually drop-in to afford maximum accessibility to its audiences. Additionally, one of the first things which visitors are greeted with upon arrival is its Children's Corner: always stocked with trails, story-kits, books and toys to help children across a range of ages engage with the collection.

However, in terms of facilities, the Museum's 1980s building was not designed with family audiences in mind: it does not have an education space in which it can host family activities; therefore all learning activities occur in the gallery among the casts. While this has limitations, for collections-care reasons, on the activities which can take place and the resources which can be used, staff consider it a positive to make family activities visible to all. The message is clear: this is a space in which families are welcome. Moreover, children may take part in activities while surrounded by the collection, and so the objects provide constant inspiration for activities. Family programming at MOCA is built around five key values, namely: positive experiences, participation, creativity, imagination, and inspiration. The following discussion expands on these values, weaving in examples of activities which the team have found successful in engaging its younger visitors.

1. Positive Experiences

It is a priority for MOCA to share knowledge of the ancient world with its visitors, no matter how young. Although the objects are not original sculptures, staff understand that the objects provide the opportunity to a meaningful encounter with the civilisations of ancient Greece and Rome. For some young people, it is their first experience of these civilisations; for others, it is a chance to build on and nurture an interest which may already have been kindled at home or at school. However, it seeks to provide means of doing this which are appropriate for informal family events which take place outside school hours. Hooper-Greenhill (2007, 36) discusses the value of learning through experiences, proposing that people learn best when they are motivated by enjoyment and that learning can take place without us realising it. It is this approach which the Museum team favours in planning family activities: interactive and engaging experiences through which children might learn by having fun. As Wu's (2007, 14) findings suggest, parents' and guardians' key motivations in visiting a museum with their family are often the enjoyment of their children and the educational benefits the visit may entail. While facilitating the discovery of the ancient world is an essential aim in programming, family events also carry a second, and no less important, objective. It is of the utmost importance to make sure that young visitors and their parents or guardians have a positive experience: that they come to see MOCA, and museums more generally, as places they feel welcome, places in which they enjoy spending time and to which they would happily return. Feedback collected at family events highlights that both nurturing an interest in the ancient world and encouraging children to see museum visits in a positive light are priorities for parents and guardians:

> This visit made the ancient Mediterranean more accessible to my kids. It may have fostered their nascent interest in the classical world. Prior to our visit, the museum did not strike me as a place for families; I am glad this notion was dispelled.

> It really excited my daughter about museums which is what I was hoping for and has encouraged me to take her to more – plus more kids events like this.

By enabling children to take part in engaging activities and to encounter friendly staff and volunteers, we hope that families will return to the Museum again. It is similarly important to give parents and guardians the confidence that activities and resources provided will help them explore the collection meaningfully with even the youngest of children and to help them feel comfortable and welcome in the museum environment – an environment which can prove stressful when managing the behaviour of young children, especially when objects are on open display, as indicated by feedback from families:

> The sculptures shouldn't be touched for conservation reasons and yet they were easy to reach to by little fingers. My little kids couldn't resist the temptation to feel the statues and demanded constant supervision and reminders.

2. Participation

Children are given the opportunity to learn through hands-on activities: this may often include making, object-handling, re-enactment and role-play. Such activities at MOCA have led to successful ways of engaging young people with the ancient world, offering an experience they will not forget. For example, at one event, children had the chance to dress up in Roman armour and to march in the footsteps of a histori-cal re-enactor. Feedback indicates that children enjoyed this active way of learning. Holding shields and wearing armour helped children to understand and have empathy for the experience of the Roman soldier, through considering questions such as how easy it was to move in the armour and how heavy the kit was with which they would have marched.

> The man outside who let the boys dress up as Romans and had artefacts to show, was great at getting them interested in history.

Another event which connected to a temporary exhibition exploring the relationship between Rome and the Indian subcontinent, offered rich opportunities for children to engage in role-play: children used replica Roman coins to purchase luxury items imported from India from volunteers posing as market traders. In order to buy the items they wanted, children had to haggle and use their powers of persuasion in an activity which boosted confidence and helped improve social skills. Through role-play, children can prepare for the real world, in which factors are constantly chang-ing, within a safe situation which they themselves have created, or helped to create (Reunamo *et al.* 2013, 304). On a different occasion, the Museum team employed a multi-sensory approach in an event which explored medicine in the ancient world: using vegetables, herbs, spices, toy mice and jelly worms, children experienced ingre-dients which may have been used in ancient cures first-hand. They discovered many of these items using their sense of smell and touch – as Schaffer (2011, 42–3) notes, young children can gain meaning and make sense of the world around them through sensory experiences. The activity also encouraged younger children to learn through play, improving manual skills, as they experimented with measuring scales and pestle and mortar, for instance.

3. Creativity

Museum events provide an excellent outlet for children's creativity and the collec-tion offers an enviable springboard for such activities. Children have made Greek temples out of cardboard, using casts from the Parthenon and Temple of Zeus at Olympia as inspiration. Not only did they learn about the architectural features of these temples, but they also designed and made their own columns, pediments and metopes to adorn their structures. This event additionally helped children to improve their problem-solving skills and spatial awareness, as they experimented with making a structurally sound model and thought about the challenges of dec-orating a triangular pediment. On some occasions the Museum team has encour-aged children to let their imagination run wild in creating their own mythological creatures, inspired by centaurs, Gorgons and satyrs among the collection; on other occasions, children have been inspired by the imperial characters discovered among the Roman portrait busts to design their own coins at the 'Roman Mint'. On others, children have made musical instruments after exploring the collection to find these lesser-spotted objects among the casts. Feedback from parents and guardians speaks positively about the opportunity to be creative and to take direct inspiration from the collection:

> The time to sit and closely observe the art, followed by the opportunity to create something inspired by it was very valuable to my daughter.

4. Imagination

At MOCA, storytelling is often used as a way to engage children: it allows the chance to tap into the imaginations of even the youngest visitors and to incorporate a sense of play – something which, for the youngest children is far from being a 'relief from serious learning' but rather 'is their way of being in this world' (Aljarrah, 2017, 26). In one storytelling event, pre-school children were able to find the hero and monsters within the story of Hercules' labours; the casts provided visual stimuli which brought the story to life, as well as a springboard from which to let their imaginations take over. Children speculated how hard it was for Hercules to hold up the world for Atlas and through play-acting with an inflatable globe, they demonstrated just how heavy they thought the world would be. They also wondered how scary the Stymphalian Birds in the story were and used craft materials to create the most terrifying bird they could dream up. The children even used musical instruments to create their own cacophony, which could rouse the birds from their nest upon hearing how Hercules startled the birds using a rattle. Feedback from parents and guardians, who attended storytelling events with their children, suggests that it serves as a positive way to access the collection for younger visitors:

> I thought it would be a good first introduction to a museum for my 4-year-old daughter (and 6-month-old son!) to spark her interest.

> A brilliantly organised story and craft event well suited for the age range it was targeted at (3–5yrs). All staff were so kind and helpful, and the storyteller captivated the imagination of the kids, wonderful! (Fig. 11.2)

5. Inspiration

Finally, MOCA seeks to inspire younger visitors through the activities they take part in. As Hooper-Greenhill (2007, 36) writes, one of the most meaningful experiences in which they might learn is through a real encounter in a real place with real things. As can be seen from feedback, the combination of a collection with the power to inspire awe in children and activities which help them to access that collection is one which can make a real impact on a child at a formative stage in their education.

> The discovery of a brilliant place where we could further explore sculpture and ancient culture. A great place to go back certainly as the children grow an interest in history, mythology, philosophy ...

Figure 11.2: Children explore the Museum at a storytelling event for families with children under 5 years old (image: Museum of Classical Archaeology, University of Cambridge).

Inspiration may come in many forms: it may ignite a passion for the ancient world, but it may instead inspire an interest in history more generally or an appetite for reading after discovering the heroes of Greek mythology; it may motivate children to think of museum visits as enjoyable and be more receptive to them in future, or it may inspire them to develop their own interests and to ask their questions about the objects they discover.

At first glance, MOCA may not strike parents and guardians as the most obvious place to bring their children. With its fragile collection, almost entirely on open display, and its prevalence of the nude human body, one can see how families may initially be nervous about paying a visit. However, the ancient world is able to offer children some of the greatest stories ever told, rich and fascinating histories, and the chance to reflect on the similarities and differences between themselves and the ancient peoples they find out about, promoting understanding and empathy with other cultures. Therefore, the Museum team will continue to rise to these challenges and to work hard both to pull out the stories and themes within the collection which will appeal to its family audience and to organise events which will spark enjoyment, creativity and imagination.

Adult Programming

It is no less important for MOCA to strive for innovative programming for its adult visitors. While some programming still takes the more traditional form of lectures and lunchtime talks, Museum staff have also experimented with 'Lates', after-hours events especially for adults, which present themselves as an alternative night out. The most comprehensive report into Lates in the UK, *A Culture of Lates* undertaken by Culture 24 (a charity supporting arts and heritage organisations), discusses the benefits of this growing trend for which there is increasing demand. Among the many benefits of Lates, the report cites the fact that they offer a chance to attract new, younger audiences, not least because they take place at a time when more adults can attend. Moreover, the themes which can be drawn from museum collections present the chance not only to educate its adult visitors but to entertain them as well (Stockman 2018). I would like to present two examples of Lates organised by the Museum, *Drink and Draw* and *Under the Fig Leaf*, which have proven popular ways for adult audiences to use its galleries as a social space after-hours and to engage with the collection in alternative ways.

1. Drink and Draw

Since 2015, MOCA has been running Drink and Draw events. Similar events have been taking place in a range of venues from galleries to bars and coffee shops across the UK and beyond for some time, but what could be more fitting a venue than the Museum's Cast Gallery, filled with hundreds of sculptures for visitors to test their artistic skills on? It can even be a playful take on the traditional art school convention of drawing from casts to practise sketching the human form. Informality is crucial to this event: Drink and Draw is intended to be accessible to all abilities, both seasoned artists and novices alike, and to invite those who may be too intimidated to join a more formal art class to exercise their creativity. Participants may choose to focus on whatever takes their fancy in the gallery and are offered a plentiful supply of drawing materials. Friendly artists circulate the space offering helpful guidance, and all participants are welcome to a complimentary drink – the organisers believe that a glass of wine will loosen up those who are unused to putting pencil to paper and will lower inhibitions a little before drawing nude sculpture.

Drink and Draw proved so popular when it was first held that it has now become a regular feature of adult programming at MOCA, with two events taking place each year. On average, around 150 people attend each event over the course of three hours – a pleasing turnout in a space with a maximum capacity of 100 people. Feedback has been overwhelmingly positive for this event. When asked what they enjoyed most, participants commented on the ambience, the opportunity to try something new and the chance to engage in a social activity in an alternative environment:

Challenging myself with new skills.

It was very relaxing just to draw freely.

Free wine. Great atmosphere. Really sociable and different.

2. Under the Fig Leaf

One of the more popular Lates held at MOCA involved choosing a theme to which organisers thought adult audiences were likely to respond well: to that end, Under the Fig Leaf was an event which explored love and sex in the ancient world, hot on the heels of Valentine's Day, and which promised audiences the opportunity to uncover the 'saucy and amorous tales' behind the casts. It was one of the most playful events the Museum had hosted for adults and involved a variety of short activities which participants could take part in throughout the evening, in addition to the novelty of simply exploring the gallery after dark. The evening included tours, led by Museum staff, whose delivery aimed to educate but to do so in a fun, light-hearted and informal manner and whose choice of content avoided heteronormativity in order to appeal to a diverse audience. A self-led scavenger hunt – an alternative to a traditional museum trail – was also on offer, which gave participants the chance to have fun exploring the collection and even afforded them licence to be a little silly in the activities, sketches and 'selfies' they were asked to complete. A Digital Maker provided a light-touch craft activity, in which participants could make greetings cards which transformed images of the casts with LED lights. This presented the opportunity for creativity, but the digital element helped ensure this activity felt suitably pitched for an adult audience. Special lighting was also arranged throughout the gallery in order to present the casts as they had rarely been seen before. For instance, the cast of the Farnese Hercules was illuminated in bright pink light, posing a challenge to his overt masculinity. As Stockman (2018, 37) suggests, 'the night time uniquely allows for the use of colour and light in a way that is less effective during the day and is a time when adults feel they can play'.

Feedback from this event indicated that visitors relished the opportunity to have fun in the Museum in an adults-only environment and enjoyed the array of activities on offer. It was also notable that participants appreciated the chance to access academic content courtesy of an expert but liked that it was presented in an alternative and whimsical manner:

> I loved the playful attitude toward the event and approaching history with fresh eyes. Having drinks, a scavenger hunt, and crafts made the entire event relaxed and memorable.

> The themed stories that also offered a glimpse into the critical discourse; the fact that it was adults only (I love children, but it's nice to have an event focused on adult learning and engagement that's also a bit fun).

Looking back to those lofty aims projected by the luminaries at the foundation of the Museum, we recall the hopes that the collection would educate the public in Classical

Archaeology, share with them the beauty of classical art, perhaps even inspiring them to nurture their own creativity. While one wonders what those VIPs would have made of the ways MOCA currently employs to engage its audience – allowing visitors to sprawl on the floor with a glass of wine, completely absorbed in sketching the casts, and inviting them to a giggle at some of the racier stories behind the sculptures, it cannot be denied that these events do fulfil the original aims of the Museum, whilst also broadening its reach, staying relevant in a shifting contemporary world, and creating an inclusive and approachable environment.

Conclusion

This paper illustrates that MOCA embraces both the challenges and the unique opportunities that a cast collection can present. Although none of its sculptures are ancient objects, the casts do provide a fantastic gateway to the ancient world, enabling programming to explore a multitude of themes including art, history, mythology, sexuality, religion and much more. As can be seen from the case studies discussed, the casts lend themselves to multiple ways of providing audiences with meaningful experiences in the Museum which offer opportunities to learn, to have fun and to develop new skills.

References

Aljarrah, A. (2017). Play as a Manifestation of Children's Imagination and Creativity. *Journal for the Education of Gifted Young Scientists* 5, 23–36.

Beard, M. (1994) Casts and Cast-offs: The Origins of the Museum of Classical Archaeology. *Proceedings of the Cambridge Philological Society* 39, 1–29.

Hooper-Greenhill, E. (2007) *Museums and Education: Purpose, Pedagogy, Performance.* Oxford, Routledge.

Reunamo, J., Lee, H-C., Wu, R., Wang, L-C., Mau, W-Y. & Lin, C.-J. (2013) Perceiving Change in Role Play. *European Early Childhood Education Research Journal* 21, 292–305.

Schaffer, S. (2011) Opening the Doors: Engaging Young Children in the Art Museum. *Art Education* 64, 40–6.

Stockman, N. (2018) A Culture of Lates: A Report into the Historic, Current And Potential Role of UK museum Lates Within the Context of the Night-time Economy. *Culture 24.* https://www.keepandshare.com/doc/8215333/a-culture-of-lates-lo-res-culture24-pdf-2-0-meg?da=y (accessed 16 February 2020).

Turner, S. (2016) *Access Policy Statement: an unpublished document from the Museum of Classical Archaeology, Cambridge.* URL: https://www.classics.cam.ac.uk/museum/museum-pdfs/policies/access-policy (accessed 20 February 2020).

Wu, K. (2007) What Do Families with Children Need from a Museum? *Cultural Policy, Criticism and Management Research 2.* URL: https://culturalpolicyjournal.files.wordpress.com/2011/05/ejournal2_wu.pdf (accessed 23 February 2020).

D. Conclusions

Chapter 12

Towards a Meaningful Discourse between Archaeology, Museums and Public Engagement

Robin Osborne

On (Not) Defining One's Public

So what public are we seeking to engage, and what are we trying to engage them in? If the papers in this collection have taught us anything it is that there is no single or simple answer to this question. As a matter of fact, Museums already engage with the public in many different guises – the young, the imprisoned, the disabled, families, artists and would be artists, music-lovers, even with the educated middle classes. As a matter of principle, there is no public with whom the museum does not want to engage. And much the same goes for what to engage them with and in, from the enchantment of technology to the shock of the skeleton, from the lure of discovery to the flash of gold, from the everyday recovered from the cess pit to the otherworldly images of gods. So is the museum trying to be all things to all people? And should it be?

At one level, there is certainly no harm in the museum extending its embrace widely and indiscriminately. There are, after all, few better places for people to spend time than a museum, where whatever they do, and however much or little time they spend reading labels, they will surely enhance their cognitive grasp on the world. But at another level danger lurks. We certainly want visitors to go away with a story but picking up inappropriate stories is all too easy. Museum displays lend themselves to appearing to tell stories about 'treasures from the past', and about archaeology as 'treasure-hunting'. The very prioritisation of the material object out of its original context that is unavoidable in a museum rightly sends shivers down archaeologists' backs. So too, visitors can easily go away with a story about the past that is romanticised and idealised, as if the exceptional materials selected by time and by museum donors, directors and curators were part of everyone's life and enjoyed as freely by all then as they are enjoyed freely today. We might wonder, here, not only about displays of jewellery or of paintings from private houses, but about the romanticising of war that comes from gleaming armouries, as in the Fitzwilliam Museum in Cambridge, or serried ranks of hoplite helmets, as in the Musée d'Art Classique at Mougins.

What the public is engaged in, and how engaged the public is, really matters. Labels carefully written in language a 12-year-old could understand fail if no one reads them. But so, too, operatic stage sets or spectacular lighting or distinctive soundtracks also fail when they are more memorable than the exhibits that they display. Casting the net widely is not the same thing as throwing out randomly into the darkness any net on which we can lay our hands. As with fish, so with 'the public', if you go out wanting to catch a particular group, you need to use a particular net and cast it in a particular place and at a particular time.

There are very good reasons for offering free classical concerts in museums during a time of economic crisis but concerts are effective bait, to change the metaphor slightly, precisely because the public inclined to go to concerts is also a public inclined to go to museums. Not only does this increase the number of visits, rather than the range of visitors, but those visitors end up seeing again the museum they already know – that is, hearing a concert is not primarily a way of changing how visitors view the museum. The danger is that they will come away with their old understandings reinforced but not questioned. There is a lot to be said for increasing the number of museum visitors who are obviously enjoying being there, for such enjoyment is infectious, but the level of public engagement with material culture is at best marginally enhanced.

The most effective public engagement projects have a very defined aim, targeting a particular group and attempting to provide that group with a particular experience: the net is precisely woven with the particular fish in mind. The work with those who are visually impaired (Chapter 10) is a good example of this. Here is a group with a very particular need and who experience the contemporary world in a very particular way. Making it possible for them to experience something of a past world in that same way, immediately enhances their perceptions not simply of the world of the museum, but of the world, period.

Such projects work because they are time-limited: resources can be devoted to one particular group for a short period that could not be devoted to that group permanently. Like the Cambridge Museum of Classical Archaeology's *Drink and Draw* or *Under the Fig Leaf* initiatives (Chapter 11), they represent a particularly well-defined version of traditional educational programmes in museums that bring in a group of more or less known characteristics and tailor the experience then shared to the needs and desires of that group. Such educational programmes appropriately adapt themselves to changing needs, whether the changes are occasioned by changing educational syllabuses or by the particular capacities of the group involved – what one does with those from an Art School and what one does with a group of students of Computer Science may need to have little in common.

But if good small group teaching in the museum, like good small group teaching elsewhere, endeavours to start from where the students already are, and to be responsive to their particular needs, that approach is not possible where engagement is with a group that cannot be so defined. As with the good public lecture, where the success of the lecturer depends upon making it possible for those starting in very different positions nevertheless all to end up with their understanding significantly changed, so good public engagement with permanent displays or short-term exhibitions depends upon those displays being able to offer something fresh, but accessible, to all.

In the case of temporary exhibitions, it is tempting for museums to settle for one design of net, maximising the catch of a single species of fish, or, in the alternative metaphor, to employ bait that is widely found attractive. Established big name artists or big name cultures (Vermeer, Troy, Banksy), and large quantities of their work, are the classic bait here, but making the design or content shocking works too, and with a different group. Those who protested at the use of human skeletons in *Krieg* will only have brought satisfaction to the exhibition curators by confirming that their desire to shock had succeeded (Chapter 6). Both strategies are good for total visitor numbers but neither is likely to produce impressive figures for diversity. More importantly, both approaches are likely to maximise engagement while minimising impact: the great majority of visitors will go away with the attitudes and cognitive awareness that they brought with them reinforced, not transformed.

In the case of permanent displays, shock is a high risk strategy that few try. The danger is that either today's shock looks pathetic, and dated, in five years' time, or that the shock is really shocking, and changes are forced by public reaction (or some particular pressure or interest group). Key pieces and famous names attract visitors to permanent displays too, though inevitably the density of famous objects and famous artists (*etc.*) that can be achieved in a permanent collection is more modest. But peddling a single narrative is not appropriate when a display needs to offer repeated visitors fresh possibilities, and remain fit for purpose over many years.

From Means to Ends: Making Knowledge Intimate

Can there be, then, a single strategy for achieving public engagement with material culture, of making archaeology truly public through museum collections? At various points in this volume, contributors lay out the principles on which they are trying to operate, or the ends which they are trying to achieve. The suggestions are that we should be starting a conversation (Chapter 4), promoting active participation and cultivating curiosity and fantasy (Chapter 9), and creating an 'interactive process and a dialectic relationship between the archaeologist, the archaeological testimony and the public' (Chapter 7), even a sense of collaboration (Chapter 9), by employing evidence-based assumptions (Chapter 8); that we should meet visitors half way, intriguing them but not baffling them and matching their mood, but that at the same time we should be implicitly or explicitly posing a question, even if not pressing a particular answer, and should be encouraging self-awareness (Chapter 6).

All these suggestions, however, are about means, and I will return to means presently. Strikingly under-represented in these papers is thought about ends. Only the authors of Chapter 2 come clean on this, suggesting that we should be aiming for 'an intimate understanding of the art and history' of the material displayed, even 'a familiarity with the essence' of the culture; that we should be cultivating respect for heritage, and at the same time using it to cultivate new skills and values. Talk of the essence of a culture may ring some alarm bells, and 'respect' may seem a low bar to aim for with regard to heritage, but 'intimate understanding' of material culture is surely the fundamental end. Finding ways to maximise the number of museum visitors who can achieve intimate knowledge is precisely what the conversations, questions, fantasy and self-awareness are means to achieve.

But what is 'intimate knowledge' when it comes to material culture? Behind the growing distance between archaeologists and museums has been a dispute about intimacy. The archaeological experience of excavation is a very intimate experience. There is a tangible sense of removing the layers accumulated by time to uncover the real past, waiting there for discovery, exactly as it was when it was deposited. That is an experience we can encourage many to share through the sorts of initiatives described in Chapter 7, but it is hard to do this in a museum. Although museums have, from time to time, experimented with replicating this, enabling young visitors to uncover objects buried in a glorified sandpit, such replication does not at all give that sense of accessing an original context, and is arguably so misleading about archaeological practice as to be more dangerous than helpful. How can it not become a game of treasure-hunting?

But is knowledge of the object in its excavated context the only sort of 'intimate knowledge'? We might concede that intimate knowledge demands knowing an object in its context, without conceding that the only context we need to know is the context where that object finally came to rest in antiquity (see Osborne 2015 and responses, especially Haggis 2018). Indeed, if we are interested in the context of the culture as a whole in which the object was created and used, then the particular context of the object's deposition (which in some cases was hundreds of years after its creation and after it had been carted off to a completely different place) does not give us the epistemic intimacy that we are looking for.

Being really intimate with an object demands more, of course, than placing it in its originating culture. The history of *e.g.* being acquired by a Roman general or trader, transferred to Rome, displayed in a Roman garden or public baths, recovered in the Renaissance, restored to become something it never was, re-restored, freed of its restorations, moved from a private collection to a museum, ensures that the object has been an intimate part of many different scenarios. In any particular display or exhibition, we may want the public to engage intimately with just one or two of those scenarios; but there is no a priori reason why knowing an object intimately in one part of its social life should be better, in any sense (epistemologically, morally, aesthetically), than knowing that object intimately in another part of its social life.

There may, however, be good reasons for thinking that it helps us become intimate with an object's social life in antiquity if we first become intimate with that object in its current context – not least because we have no choice but to acknowledge that current context. Being explicit about the epistemology of the museum display can only be a good thing.

But how do we make the public intimate with any object in any of its contexts? It is easy to think of aspects of intimacy that cannot be shared. Normally we cannot become intimate with ancient objects by touch (even with modern replicas like plaster casts, that is an issue) (see Chapter 10), nor by using them for their initial purposes. That deprives us of registering the smoothness or coldness of a surface, the weight or balance of a drinking vessel, the ease or difficulty of pouring from a storage vessel, the technique of extracting drops of oil from a stirrup jar, the humour of trick vases and so on. Nor can we have much sense of the auditory quality of ancient objects – what cups sounded like when they touched one another; how different the sound was when an amphora of wine was emptied into a bronze dinos or crater rather than into a ceramic one. None of those life experiences, which were no doubt part of what it was to grow up and become cultured in the relevant ancient society, is available to us – some of them not even to museum professionals.

The Senses of Intimacy

Although it is good to remind ourselves from time to time of how partial anyone's intimacy with past societies and cultures is, it does not make sense to dwell on, or obsess over, what is completely lost or hard to acquire. It is true that of our five traditional senses only sight and in some circumstances hearing are, in most museum contexts, going to be employed in acquiring our intimate knowledge, but those are the senses through which we acquire most knowledge, not only of past worlds but also of the current world. Film, television and the forms of virtual contact many of us resorted to in order to maintain our social distance during the present Covid-19 pandemic, all deprive us of smell, feel and taste, and even in the case of sound, they privilege the sound of the human voice over the sounds of the surrounding world. The greater the intimate knowledge of antiquity that we learn to acquire through sight, the greater our intimate knowledge will be of the world we inhabit.

Archaeologists and Art Historians (at least when they are doing Art History) contrast to Historians precisely in their privileging of observation. Where Historians, Social Scientists and literary scholars privilege text (albeit more normally text read than text heard), Archaeologists and Art Historians, like the best of Social Anthropologists, privilege things seen. It is by observing visual patterning – in the earth, on distribution maps, across artefacts and the images on artefacts – that both Archaeologists and Art Historians operate. There are big arguments among Archaeologists about whether the Art Historian's observations tell something valuable or not, but visitors cannot even begin to be introduced to the debate unless they are given some idea of what it is to view like an Art Historian. The challenge in the museum is how to convey the intimate knowledge that Archaeologists and Art Historians acquire by observing in the way that they do, how to make the visitor see with the Archaeologist's or Art Historian's eye.

It is ironic that although we derive so much of our experience of the world from (silent, scentless – and sometimes, of course, tasteless) images, whether still or moving, teaching and learning has long privileged the spoken and written word. For all that people actually learn by observation, they are conditioned to expect that they learn by hearing or reading. There is certainly intimate knowledge of the material culture of antiquity, of the social life of things (to use the phrase wonderfully coined by Appadurai (1986)), to be obtained (only) from literary and non-literary texts. There is also a necessary place for text, whether audible or silently read, in directing visual observation within the museum. But what sort of text?

There is a good reason why so much of the discussion of means in the chapters of this volume has been about establishing a conversation, cultivating curiosity and fantasy, making the visitor a collaborator in an interactive process. 'Active learning' has long been shown superior to passive learning. The best small group teaching has the teacher pose questions for the students to think about in relation to knowledge already acquired or immediately available to them, and then refines the student's answer to get the student to incorporate more factors and make more connections. Curators are told to avoid questions in their labels, for fear of frustrating visitors or making them feel stupid, but the problem comes not from asking questions, but from not providing the means to answer them. Again, like a good teacher, by the time the question is asked, how to answer it should be obvious. Being made to ask questions one would not otherwise ask is a way of coming to see from a different angle, and it is in coming to see an object or event from a wide variety of angles that one acquires intimate knowledge.

The Storied Past

Just as historians traditionally enticed their readers in by the excitement of a well-con-structed narrative that enabled the reader to see how one thing led to another, so museums have traditionally encouraged their visitors by a broadly chronological dis-play to see similarly how one thing led to another, sometimes helping to simplify the story by separating artefacts of different types (ceramics from sculpture from work in precious metal) or made in different places (doing British art separately from European art separately from Japanese art). What a good 'hang' has done is juxtapose works of art in such a way that similarities and differences emerge, and the viewer acquires a sense of the differences between individual artists and between successive periods of art. Labels have been limited to identifying the painting and its artist and giving its date. Penelope Curtis's recent rehang of galleries at Tate Britain returned to this mode of engaging visitors, with a more strictly chronological display.

There are contexts in which such an historical narrative remains both the most straightforward and the most important way of engaging any public. This is not only the principle behind Museums whose current arrangement was established long ago, like the National Archaeological Museum in Athens (Chapter 9), but of more recently established displays too, such as the Museum of Classical Archaeology in Cambridge (Chapter 11), laid out by Anthony Snodgrass in the 1980s, or the New Acropolis Museum. The description of the display in Chipperfield's rebuilt Neues Museum in Chapter 3 explains how that museum has once more adopted a display that divides by time and by region; similarly, for all its innovative use of three dimensions in a single case, the 'Cambridge wall' of the Museum of Archaeology and Anthropology, discussed in Chapter 4, also basically takes a region and divides by time. The great attraction of such a narrative is that it gives the visitor a sense of becoming part of an evolving cultural community – exactly what a National Museum or a local museum, in particular, wishes to promote.

But therein lies also the problem. These narratives end up over-stating internal factors in cultural change, giving the impression of separate cultural islands all developing independently. This idea of independent development not only falsifies what really happened in the past but also suggests that cultural independence and cultural purity are what has produced exhibition-worthy arts and crafts in the past, and that they are to be valued for their own sakes. Nor is this a problem solved by adding in to the display a few key items from another culture to show them to be catalysts of change, for such a tactic only fuels models of 'waves of influence' or promotes a view of the course of cultural history being changed by a single genius.

One reason why new techniques of public engagement are needed, beyond the attractions of the exciting narrative of whiggish progress, is that the story with which we wish to engage the public is a more complicated story, and the skills which we wish to impart more fundamental skills than merely the ability, desirable though it is, to situate a particular item of material culture in its place and time. We want our visitors to ask of a painting not merely how it relates in its technique and composition to other works of the place and period, but why it displays that subject in that way. We want our visitors not merely to recognise that particular shape of amphora as distinctive of those produced in a particular Roman province over a particular period but to ask what it was about that shape that caused it to be adopted at that time, and what it was about Roman trade that led to amphorae of that shape being found wherever the given example was found. We want our visitors to see in yet another torso of Venus not just how what Greek sculptures of the 4th and 3rd centuries BC looked like and why they, in particular, came to be replicated and distributed across the Roman Empire as a sign of belonging to the ruling culture, but how a particular model of gender relations was imported with this Venus and to ask what local tensions importing that model brought. We want them to come to see all that by comparing and contrasting what is before them with other items that they know or can be shown, whether in the same case or gallery or on an information board or app.

Temporary exhibitions, as discussed in Chapter 6, are able to tell more complicated stories – though they do not always choose to do so – because they can be designed and set up for a single purpose. Permanent galleries do not have that luxury. The questions that they pose have to be sufficiently clear and the stories they offer sufficiently coherent, even to those passing through rapidly, to suggest to the visitor that spending a bit more time in the gallery, and paying attention to more of the information provided, will be rewarded. Given that galleries have little choice but to start where at least a substantial proportion of their public expect them to start, the challenge is how to disrupt their progress sufficiently to make them ask different questions, and see the material differently, in the course of their visit.

One way of doing this is to include some objects which so obviously do not 'fit' the story that seems to be emerging as to make the visitor reassess how adequate that story is – that is, to disrupt the coherence but not sufficiently to undermine the initial impression that there is a clear and coherent story. In terms of small group teaching, this is the technique of 'letting the cat out of the bag' – introducing some new consideration or new piece of evidence that challenges the answer that is being formulated.

The most straightforwardly available supply of objects that do not 'fit' is the gallery itself, with disruption to the straightforward story introduced by offering visitors a variety of ways around the display, encouraging them not simply to review each case from left to right and then move on clockwise around the gallery, but to divert in order to see something similar or linked, or indeed contrasting, in another case or another part of the gallery. This is a familiar enough technique in terms of 'museum trails' but is rarely employed for adult visitors or to raise fundamental issues of interpretation.

The fundamental need is to get the public engaged in a story that they find compelling. Any story requires some text, if only to make it possible for the story to be retold by the visitor without the objects before them. More complicated stories inevitably demand more text, and so the challenge is to get the visitor to engage beyond the level of the label. The discussion of the handlist and the app. used in the Cambridge Museum of Archaeology and Anthropology, in Chapter 4, nicely reveals the extent of the challenge here. Apps turn out not to command any longer attention span than physical text, although they have the advantage of enabling us to measure that attention span.

Promoting Conversation

There is one form of text which consistently engages the public for significant periods and that is the live text of a guide. Live guides inevitably vary in quality but there is no doubt that delivering text in a way that enables the text to be received simultaneously with looking at the object that is the subject of the text is the most effective way of linking what is seen to information about it. The successive glance from label or bread board or hand-sheet or phone app. to object and back demands much more concentration, and often demands that the visitor already knows quite a lot about the object in question, even to match the description on the label to the object in front of them. It is the immediacy with which information perceived orally can be applied to what is seen with the eyes that recommends the ever-popular audio guides, used in the Neues Museum (Chapter 3), and the audio clips that were a popular part of the Cambridge Museum of Archaeology and Anthropology app. (Chapter 4).

Yet audio guides are regularly poorly used. In a common version, the visitor keys in a number to be presented with a more discursive version of what the label to the object says. Although stories may be told about individual objects, this version of the audio guide often offers nothing by way of a narrative about the display as a whole, let alone a more complicated story than the information boards and labels can tell. But if the visitor is to understand not just some facts about some objects, but why objects/works of art like that were made/used at that place and time, then they need not a set of stories but an overall story.

The good Archaeology or Art History lecture is something other, and more, than a series of descriptions of objects, end-to-end; so too the good guide, whether live or recorded, ought to be doing more than sequential description and labelling. There is no reason at all for not drawing the listener's attention to objects elsewhere in a gallery that shed more and different light upon material that is currently being viewed or allow different questions to be asked about that material, or different answers to be given. Good stories have suspense, but they also employ anticipation. Good guides notice what has caught the imagination of the visitors they are talking to, and pick that up and play on it, always taking the visitor on from where they have got to, responding to, and indeed anticipating their questions.

Archaeology is a critical discourse that is all about stories that ask and answer questions. While properly wishing to squeeze as much information as possible from the context in which an object is found, it is a fundamental part of archaeology to recognise that that context itself, as well as the object, has a history. For the archaeologist, what intimate knowledge means is knowledge of the social life of the object prior to deposition, as well as its life as deposited. The social life of things was, and is, as varied as the social life of people – just in many cases rather longer. When we see an object in a museum what we are seeing is something rather like a person cut out of a photograph. The great advantage of cutting away the particular background from a person in a photograph is that it removes distraction, removes a particular moment of their social life, and allows the person to be put in different contexts and given a different social life. The great disadvantage is that no one ever exists without a context, a social life. And for the object in the museum the great danger is that the museum case becomes the only context, as if the social life of this antiquity involved only being a pin-up for the museum-goer's gaze.

Conventional audio guides remain a great way to get visitors to use the knowledge they already have, or knowledge that can be gained from elsewhere in the gallery, as well as giving a chance to hear the voice of an expert or an excavator or other evocative soundscape. But when it comes to introducing things unfamiliar to the visitor that are outside the gallery, or indeed simply to making it much easier to find other objects elsewhere in the gallery smart phone apps clearly have greater potential still, since they give the possibility of offering images, as well as sound. They also give easier possibilities of offering and showing alternative routes, or possibilities of burrowing down to different degrees, to allow for visitors whose existing knowledge is different. But there is a delicate balance here: one wants the phone to spend most of its time in the visitor's pocket with the visitor listening on earphones, while their visual attention is on the objects in the gallery. If the phone itself end ups being what the visitor spends their time staring at then the object itself ends up excluded from the conversation.

Conclusion

This book has shown how much thought and attention has been devoted, over the past decade or so, to increasing public engagement in the museum. The 'here it is, take it or leave it' approach of museums up to a generation ago has been replaced by a concern to ensure that visitors of all sorts are enabled to 'take it'. That has affected exhibition and gallery design, the wording of labels, breadboards, information panels, and hand-lists or catalogues. It has led to much more happening in galleries, whether in terms of otherwise attractive activities (*e.g.* concerts) or in terms of interventions designed to bring out unexpected aspects of exhibits. Museums now have much less hesitation with starting from the visitors and their experiences, categories, and questions, rather than starting from the past cultures and prioritising what Archaeologists take to be their categories.

Inevitably, galleries and exhibitions, like good teachers, need to tell a story and set an agenda. But if they only tell one story (as it were 'the story of money'), they are almost inevitably going to end up patronising some visitors and baffling others (*cf.* Chapter 13). The trick has to be to turn visitors from passive recipients of knowledge into active learners, learners able to shape the story they receive according to their own prior knowledge, understanding, and interests. To turn the visitors themselves into archaeologists and art historians, we need to put them into a position where they can puzzle for themselves over the objects they see, and come to understand how they themselves can use comparison and contrast, both within the particular exhibition case and gallery and more broadly, to answer the questions of what that object was and did, has been and has done, is and does, that they (are prompted to) ask. They will not acquire on a single visit, staring at objects behind glass, the intimate knowledge that the archaeologist or art historian has, but at least they will understand what it would be to have that intimate knowledge.

Museum collections started without labels, reliant upon visitors conversing with knowledgeable guides. In an ideal world one might return to that – for what could be more engaging? But the voyage of discovery constituted by the 18th-century candlelit tour can now be replicated, and replicated in ways that oblige the visitor to take an active role in directing the voyage. There is some way to go in learning what can be managed, and managed on a reasonable expenditure of time and money, but the technology is now available to enable a decisive step forward.

References

Appadurai, A. (1986) *The Social Life of Things: Commodities in Cultural Perspective*. Cambridge, Cambridge University Press.

Haggis, D. (2018) Discussion and Debate: In Defense of a Contextual Classical Archaeology. *Journal of Mediterranean Archaeology* 31, 101–19.

Osborne, R. (2015) De-contextualising and Re-contextualising: Why Mediterranean Archaeology Needs to get out of the Trench and Back Into the Museum. *Journal of Mediterranean Archaeology* 28, 241–61.